PENNY DOWDELL

Embroidered INTERIORS

Stitch 11 Charming Spaces • Skill Building Techniques

stashBOOKS®
an imprint of C&T Publishing

Publisher: Amy Barrett-Daffin

Creative Director: Gailen Runge

Senior Editor: Roxane Cerda

Editor: Madison Moore

Technical Editor: Sarah Ruiz

Cover/Book Designer: April Mostek

Production Coordinator: Tim Manibusan

Illustrator: Kirstie Pettersen

Photography Coordinator: Rachel Ackley

Front cover and Lifestyle photography by Duncan Longden

Instructional Photography by Penny Dowdell, unless otherwise noted

Published by Stash Books, an imprint of C&T Publishing, Inc., P.O. Box 1456, Lafayette, CA 94549

Library of Congress Cataloging-in-Publication Data

Names: Dowdell, Penny, 1994- author

Title: Embroidered interiors : stitch 11 charming spaces; skill-building techniques / Penny Dowdell.

Description: Lafayette, CA : Stash Books, an imprint of C&T Publishing, [2026] | Summary: "Discover the art of embroidery like never before with Embroidered Interiors-your guide to stitching detailed, lifelike home spaces. Explore various stunning room patterns, including a botanical conservatory, a kitchen full of lively characters, and more. Plus, choose from a unique collection of mix-and-match pattern pieces to help you on your journey"-- Provided by publisher.

Identifiers: LCCN 2025030236 | ISBN 9781644035870 trade paperback | ISBN 9781644035887 ebook

Subjects: LCSH: Embroidery | Embroidery--Patterns

Classification: LCC TT770 .D653 2026 | DDC 746.44--dc23/eng/20250820

LC record available at https://lccn.loc.gov/2025030236

Printed in China

10 9 8 7 6 5 4 3 2 1

Dedication

For Nan, Nana, and Big Sarah

Acknowledgements

I am deeply grateful to everyone who contributed to the creation of this book. Special thanks to my editor Madison and the entire team at C&T Publishing—your guidance and encouragement convinced me this project was possible. My sincere appreciation goes to photographer Duncan Longden for bringing my visual concepts to life with such skill.

To my family—Mum, Dad, Saz, and Heather—thank you for your steadfast support through many video calls filled with stitching sessions. Jo, your attentive ear and enthusiastic feedback were invaluable.

Above all, my heartfelt gratitude to Austin, my partner and greatest advocate. You listened patiently to every idea, assisted with photography and materials, provided unwavering support when challenges seemed insurmountable, and kept me fueled with coffee and snacks throughout the writing process. I couldn't have done it without you!

CONTENTS

Introduction

I'm so excited that you've picked up this book! Embroidery is a centuries-old craft, but the projects in this book are all about making embroidery playful, modern, and enjoyable.

I grew up surrounded by little arts and crafts projects. My nan taught me how to knit, a dear family friend gave me her sewing machine, and my dad brought home old haberdashery items and bedsheets for me to turn into dodgy dresses or lopsided ornaments. At school, I loved art class and had amazing teachers who expanded my knowledge of textiles and the creative process.

Studying fashion at university was a dream come true. I loved researching and creating my own thoughtful designs, which often featured textiles and handicraft skills. However, after leaving university I no longer had access to important tools or opportunities to create large scale work.

By chance, I had a couple of embroidery hoops in a drawer. I stitched a wonky quote onto black felt as a Christmas gift for someone. It felt nice to work small and hold the hoop in my hands as I watched the design come to life. That lit a fire which has now been burning for ten years! My walls quickly filled up with finished hoops. To my delight, I launched a simple website and was amazed to receive my first orders.

Since then, my design style has evolved and developed. When I left England in 2018 to live in Taiwan with my partner, I took only a sparse embroidery kit with me, having no idea if it would be something I continued. But in a new culture and environment, it became an essential practice to bring me peace and connection.

Then, interior design emerged in my work. Being in a strange new place revealed to me the importance of the spaces we live in. Our homes are not only safe havens in which to relax and unwind, but are also spaces in which we can release our personalities! In my work, I've stitched recreations of houses I've lived in, but also created new dream spaces with a needle and thread. It's a little like playing with a dollhouse, painting the walls and rearranging furniture and trinkets into new and exciting rooms!

How to Use This Book

This book begins with a comprehensive introduction to all the materials, methods, and stitches you will need to complete the projects in this book. I advise reading through it before starting on the projects.

Each room project is made of three things: the box of the room (walls, floor and ceiling), the furniture, and the details. The projects in this book depict ten imaginary rooms. They feature vibrant color palettes, a range of stitches, and many interesting details. They all have a similar creation process: stitching outlines first, and then filling in the color. Using outlines and block color work makes the designs look like illustrations. They're almost like coloring pages!

Importantly, each project focuses on a different technique or skill that can be applied to any piece of embroidery art. Some teach you new stitches, while others incorporate a range of unique materials. Each project comes with templates.

The projects can be stitched in any order. The step-by-step instructions will guide you through every part of the process. There are also personalization ideas at the end of each project that encourage you to make the design more unique to you! Finally, there is a special chapter that teaches you to create your own mix-and-match pattern design using a selection of more than 25 elements.

Join me in stitching up your own dimensional dream home!

Tools and Materials

You don't need much to get started with embroidery, which is one of the best things about this craft! All the essential haberdashery items you'll need can be found in craft shops, online, or even secondhand. There are plenty of other tools and gadgets on the market, and as you progress in your embroidery journey, you'll be able to figure out what makes your life easier, and what is unnecessary.

For the best results and the easiest process, start with good quality materials. A wonky hoop or unsuitable fabric could cause you big headaches for your projects. And embroidery should be enjoyable!

Hoops

One of the best things you can do for your embroidery is choose the right hoop. A good quality hoop keeps your fabric properly stretched, sits comfortably in your hands while you work, and has smooth edges that won't snag your threads. Embroidery hoops come in a variety of sizes: the size refers to the diameter, which is usually listed in centimeters or inches (be sure to check which!). Some popular, good quality hoop brands are Nurge, Elbesee, and Hardwicke Manor.

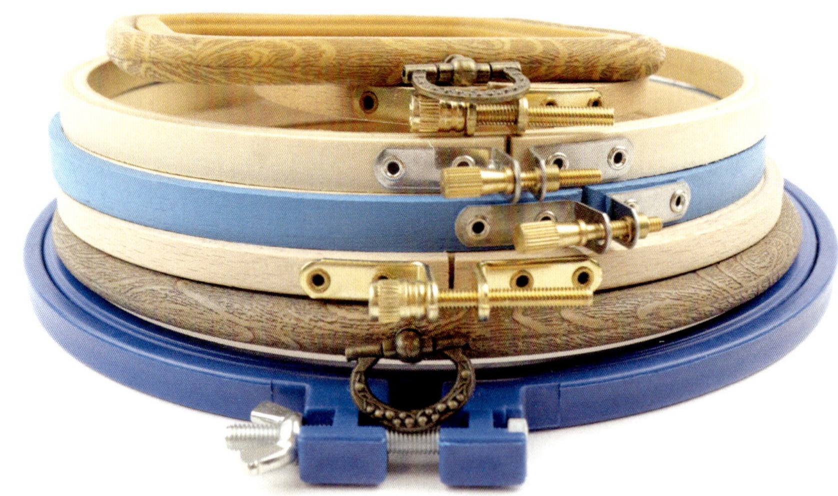

DMC
310 12
Pentel Arts
ACRYLIC COLOR
28ml

HOOP MATERIAL

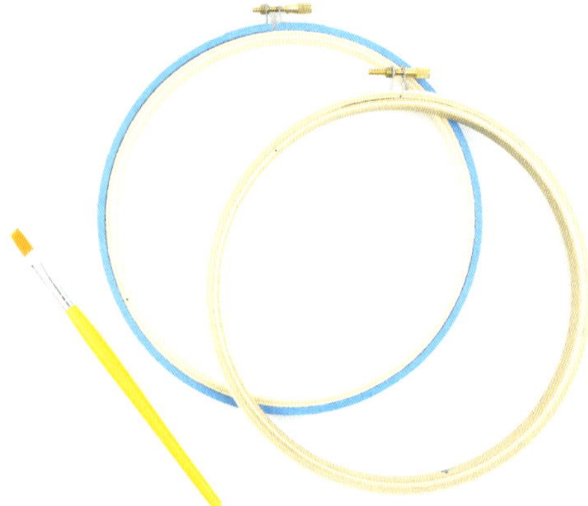

Wooden embroidery hoops are the most popular, and are generally the best to use. Make sure that the inner and outer hoops fit together with no gaps or buckles. Look for bamboo or beechwood. Some wooden hoops are treated or varnished, which can give a nice look. Or, if you buy an unvarnished hoop, you can varnish it or paint it an interesting color with acrylic paint.

Rigid plastic hoops are often brightly colored, which might work for displaying your design, and they usually keep good fabric tension. If you want to display the piece in a hoop that doesn't have very good tension (like a pretty wooden one), you could stitch in a plastic hoop and then transfer the finished project to the wooden one.

Soft rubber hoops, which usually have a wood effect finish, look cool but are not good for stitching, as they don't keep the fabric tight. Again, if you want to use a hoop like this for displaying your final embroidery piece, use a rigid hoop for stitching, and then transfer the project.

The screw fastening at the top for tightening is also important. They usually come in gold or silver finish. Tightening the bolts with your fingers will usually be enough, but if you're struggling with getting enough tension, get screws that can be used with a screwdriver and tightened further.

HOOP SHAPE & SIZE

The designs in this book are all for round hoops, as this is the most common hoop shape. You can also buy oval or square hoops and tweak the designs to fit if you want to experiment.

The designs in this book are 7″ or 8″ (18 or 20cm). This size is comfortable to work with in your hands and big enough to include lots of detail, but not so big that it becomes uncomfortable to hold. You can enlarge, reduce, or crop the designs to fit in your chosen hoop.

Fabric

It's essential to choose the right fabric. If you're unsure about whether a fabric is suitable for stitching a design, practice stitching on it first with a small hoop. Woven fabric, often called non-stretch fabric, is the best option for stitching. Look for linens, cottons, or cotton-linen blends. Wash and iron the fabric before using it in case of shrinkage.

Woven fabrics can have different thicknesses and can vary by how tightly they are woven. A medium-weight, tight-woven fabric will maintain tension while you stitch and be easy to stitch through. Thicker fabrics will be harder to stitch through, and thin fabrics may slip around in the hoop. If you are using a thin fabric, consider stitching on two layers. I stitched a lot of the designs in this book onto beige cotton-linen. The neutral color is easy to transfer a design onto.

TIP • You should consider which transfer method you want to use when deciding which fabric to use (see Transfer Methods, page 18).

Some of the projects in this book call for **patterned fabric**. Consider the scale of the fabric print compared to the size of the hoop and the design. For example, what may seem like small flowers on a large piece of fabric will look like big flowers in a small embroidery hoop! Large-scale prints may look abstract or lose their overall design when only a small section is visible in the hoop.

TIP • Avoid knit fabrics, as their stretchy quality will distort your embroidery. Knit fabrics are also called stretch fabrics. T-shirt or jersey material are common examples.

Felt fabric is great for backing a finished hoop (see Display and Finishing, page 36). It can vary in blend, thickness, and stretch. The best felt for crafting is a wool blend felt, which is usually a blend of wool with synthetic fibers such as rayon or acrylic. This makes it soft, durable, and less expensive than 100% wool.

Felt comes in various thicknesses, but the best for crafting is about ⅛″ (3mm). For felt with a little (but not too much) stretch, aim for around 0.25 g/cm^3.

Unbranded craft felt (that will usually be perfect to use) can be found in most art and textile stores, but Benzie Design (US) is also a good place to look for their wide range of colors.

Needles

Each project specifies which hand-sewing embroidery needle you should stitch with. But, at the end of the day, you should stitch with a needle that feels comfortable in your hand.

The number associated with a needle size refers to the thickness of the needle (smaller numbers are thicker needles). For regular pearl and six-strand embroidery thread, use a needle with medium thickness. Use thin needles for threading tiny beads and thick needles for stitching with yarn or crewel cotton. Starting with a variety pack, like DMC embroidery needles in sizes 3–9, will give you enough options to figure out which needle size you prefer. If you are stitching with thicker threads such as tapestry wool or Eco Vita organic yarn, you will probably need thicker tapestry needles, which range from sizes 22–28 and are blunter.

If you struggle with threading needles, look for a needle threader or self-threading needles. You might also want to get a needle minder, which is a fun magnetic accessory that keeps your needle safe when you're not stitching.

Needle threader

Needle minder

Threads

All the projects in this book use DMC threads (also called floss), and the color numbers match the official DMC color codes. DMC threads do not fade or discolor over time, and they are high-quality across all types and varieties. They are smooth and much less prone to knotting than cheaper threads. Pull the loose strand at the bottom of the skein (the side with the barcode/numbers on the label) when starting a skein to avoid making a knot.

TIP • **If you cannot access DMC thread, Anchor and Olympus are two good alternative brands. You can find color conversion charts online to match the colors.**

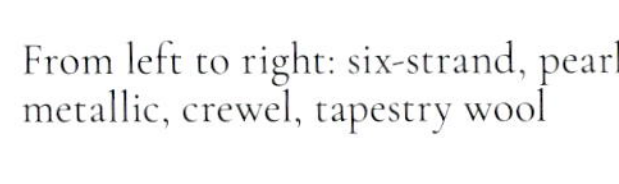

From left to right: six-strand, pearl, metallic, crewel, tapestry wool

SIX-STRAND FLOSS

The most commonly used thread is DMC Mouliné Six Strand Embroidery Floss. It comes in 8.7 yd (8m) skeins, and there is a huge array of colors. You can separate the 6-strands to stitch. Most designs in this book call for 3 strands (see Splitting Thread, page 19).

PEARL THREAD

Pearl thread (also called perle) is slightly thicker cotton thread. It comes as 1 strand, in a skein or ball. Pearl thread is used for stitching the outlines in all the projects of this book. When purchasing pearl thread, pay attention to the color code and the thickness code. I always recommend thickness #12 in this book.

METALLIC THREAD

Metallic thread can be the most daunting to stitch with because it can be prone to knots, but it's always worth it for the sparkly highlights! Like classic six-strand thread, metallic thread can also be separated into 6-strands. You'll usually only need one or two strands at a time (see Splitting Thread, page 19).

CREWEL THREAD

Crewel thread is a thin, non-separating wool thread. It comes in 8.7 yd (8m) skeins. The DMC Eco Vita line (used in the Cozy Crewel Study, page 100) has a beautiful selection of soft, muted colors.

TAPESTRY WOOL

While tapestry wool isn't used in the projects in this book, you might like to try it out for really chunky stitching.

TIP • Thread cards can be a useful way to organise threads and keep them neat. Just be sure to write the thread number on the card when you wind the thread onto it.

Scissors

Use fabric scissors to cut fabric down to size. Pinking shears are a nice addition to your toolbox, as they will cut a zig-zag line that prevents fabric edges from fraying. You might also need paper scissors for cutting the patterns. Don't cut paper with fabric scissors; you will blunt them!

Embroidery snips are small scissors that are handy for quickly snipping thread while you stitch. They also come in a variety of cute and fun designs to bring more joy to your stitching experience!

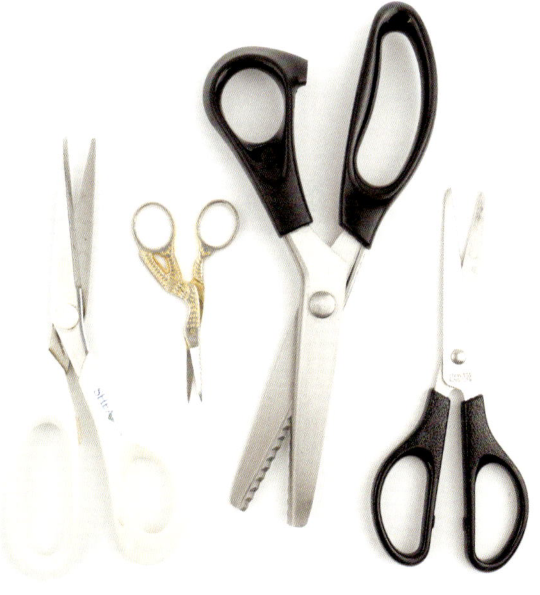

Glue

White craft glue is used in several of the projects. It's important to get a glue that dries clear and sticks to fabric well. Most craft glues will work well, or look for brands such as Elmer's or UHU. White craft glue is also known as PVA glue. If you are unsure about a certain glue, test it out on spare fabric first!

You might want to use a paintbrush to apply the glue. Make sure to wash the paintbrush with water immediately after use, before the glue dries.

Studio Set-Up

It is worth considering where you will sit to work and embroider. Of course, if you are taking your embroidery traveling, this isn't as important. But if you plan to stitch regularly at home, it's a good idea to create a well-lit and comfortable space for yourself. Care for your back and your eyes! My studio is full of light (windows for daylight, multiple lamps for the evening), a comfortable chair, and plenty of inspiration on the walls and all around!

HOOP STAND

A hoop stand is not essential, but it is worth considering. They can be useful to avoid back pain, depending on how and where you sit to embroider. There are various makes and models available depending on your posture and set-up.

Iron

It's always a good idea to wash and iron your fabric before using it, particularly if you are going to use wash-away pattern transfer paper. You don't want your stitching to shrink after your piece is finished!

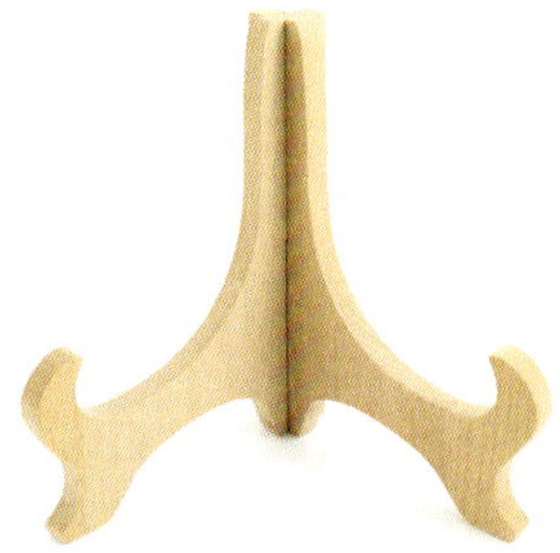

Travel Bag

If you plan on taking your embroidery on the go with you (a wonderful idea, by the way!), you'll need to take essential tools with you and keep the hoop safe from harm.

Find a fairly flat bag big enough for the hoop and ideally with a bit of structure or thickness so the hoop is more protected. If possible, a bag with pockets is great so you can store threads and tools separate from the project. Laptop bags or iPad cases are perfect for this. Even some make-up bags work great!

ESSENTIAL TOOLS

- Hoop with fabric loaded and pattern transferred
- Thread snips
- Threads (that you'll need for the trip or day)
- Color guide (or photo of color guide)
- Small bag for thread waste
- Needles (take a spare just in case)

Display Methods

Think about how you want to display your finished embroidery. If you decide to keep the piece in the embroidery hoop, you can hang it by the screw or display it on a stand. You could also frame the hoop in a shadow box frame. Finally, you can take the piece out of the hoop and display it in a cute frame! Whatever you decide, it's great to make a plan for displaying your piece.

Project-Specific Tools and Materials

Many of the projects require specific supplies that are key to that design. Each project will outline the specifics of these unique materials. Make sure you review the project you want to stitch before you go shopping!

Transfer Tools

Transfer Methods (page 18) outlines two ways of transferring a pattern to the fabric. I suggest reviewing your options before purchasing transfer tools. Depending on your preferred methods, you may need wash-away pattern paper, a lightbox, a Frixion or fineline erasable pen, pins, and a ruler. I recommend Sulky Stick 'n Stitch Stabilizer paper or C&T Publishing Wash-Away Stitch Stabilizer.

Preparing to Stitch

Prepare the Hoop

1. Wash, dry and iron the fabric. Cut the fabric to the size as instructed by the project instructions. Examine the grain of the woven fabric, and cut straight (so the grain runs horizontal and vertical). **A B**

2. Place the fabric centered on top of the inner hoop so the grain runs straight. Place the loosely screwed outer hoop over the fabric and inner hoop. **C D**

3. Start to tighten the hoop screw (either by hand or with a screwdriver), while pulling the fabric outside the hoop around the whole perimeter. **E**

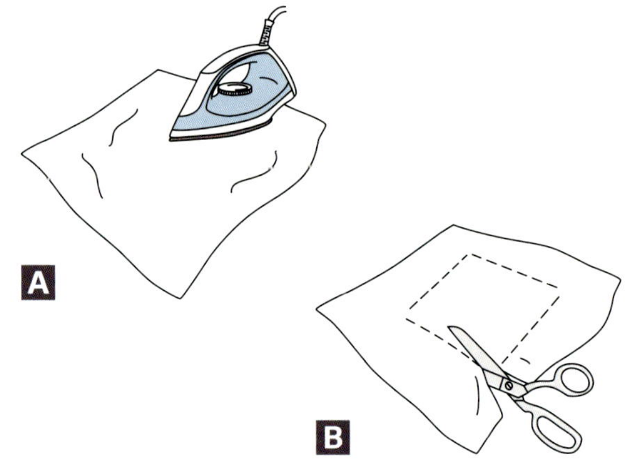

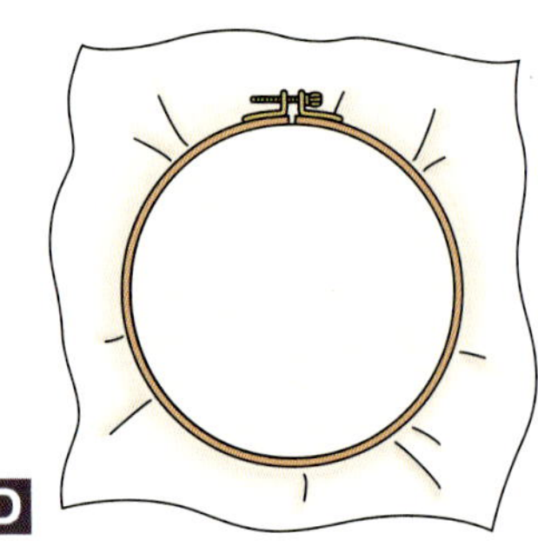

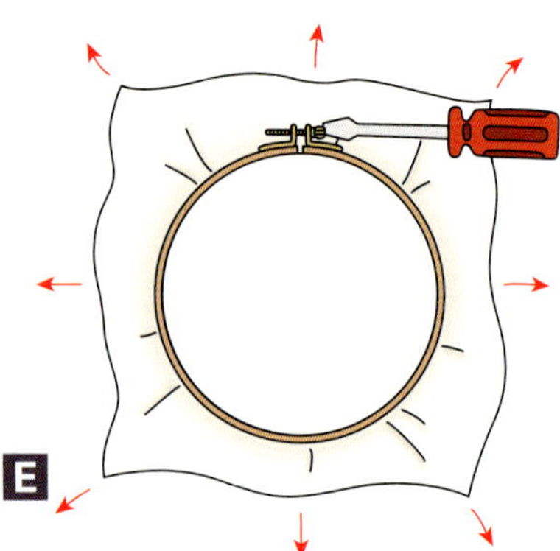

ACRYLIC COLOR
Pentel Arts
TAPISSERIE
TAPESTRY
TAPICERIA
6 AIGUILLES
NEEDLES · AGUJAS
D·M·C
22

Transfer Methods

There are many different ways to transfer the designs onto fabric. I prefer the wash-away paper method, and use it for all the projects in this book. You can research lots of other innovative ways beyond the two explained here. Tracing paper is an option, or you could stiffen the fabric with a temporary backing, and print directly onto it if you have a suitable printer.

WASH-AWAY TRANSFER PAPER METHOD

This method is the best for transferring detailed patterns. It also is the best way to transfer a design onto dark or patterned fabric. I recommend using Sulky Stick 'n Stitch Stabilizer or C&T Publishing Wash-Away Stitch Stabilizer, which come in A4 or letter-sized sheets that can be printed onto.

1. Copy or print the pattern onto the wash-away transfer paper. Print onto the fabric/stabilizer side—not the backing paper. Cut the pattern out, leaving a ⅜″ (1cm) border. **A**

2. Peel the backing paper away, and carefully stick onto the fabric in the prepared hoop. **B**

3. Stitch the outline of the pattern (as directed by the project) through the fabric and the paper. If any sticky residue builds up on the needle, wipe the needle with a damp cloth and dry before continuing to stitch.

4. When the outline stitching is complete, take the fabric out of the hoop and wash away the dissolvable paper under a faucet or in a bowl of water. Make sure the paper is completely dissolved, especially from detailed areas where there is a lot of stitching. **C**

4. Press away the excess water with a towel, then allow to dry flat. Don't wring the fabric. Iron on the back side of the fabric. **D**

5. Load the fabric back in the hoop with the design centered, and tighten again, making sure the lines of stitching are straight and not distorted.

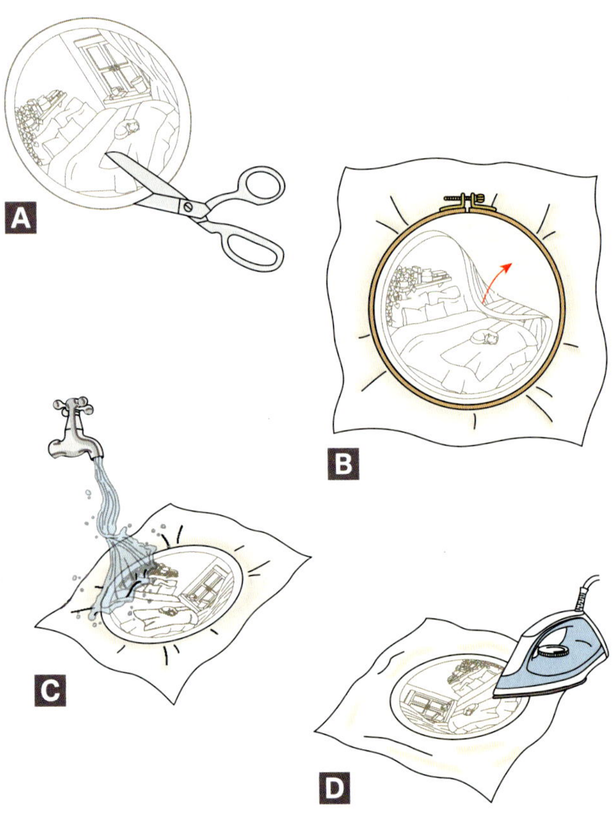

TRACE METHOD

This method doesn't require special materials, so it's convenient, especially when you're first getting started. The thickness and color of the fabric and the quality of the backing light will affect the viability of this method. Print or copy the pattern onto paper. You also need an erasable fineline pen (like a Frixion pen), a ruler, pins, and a light source (window, tablet, or lightbox).

1. Load the fabric into the hoop with the wrong/back side of the fabric facing up. Then, turn the hoop over so the flat (wrong) side of fabric lies flush with the pattern. The right side of the fabric will now be visible, under the inner hoop. Pin the pattern and fabric together. **A**

2. Using a light source from behind the hoop, trace the design onto the fabric using the erasable pen. **B**

TIP • You can choose to use a non-erasable fineline pen or a sharp pencil since the lines will be covered by stitching.

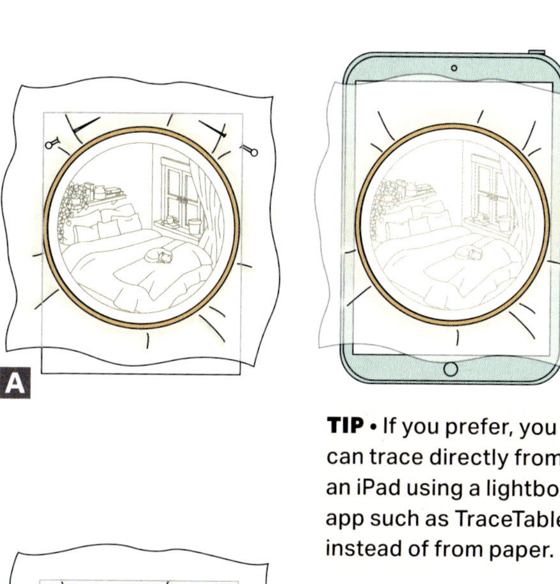

TIP • If you prefer, you can trace directly from an iPad using a lightbox app such as TraceTable instead of from paper.

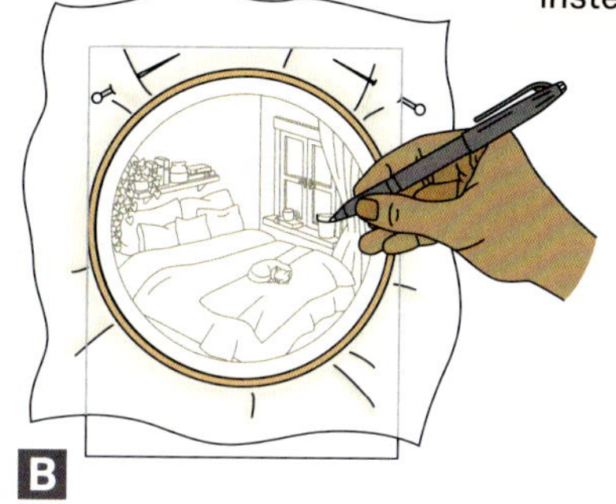

3. Unpin the pattern, and take the fabric out of the hoop. Flip the fabric and reload it onto the hoop so the traced design on the right side of the fabric is at the front. **C**

4. If there are many straight lines in the design, go over the lines with a ruler to ensure everything is straight. **D**

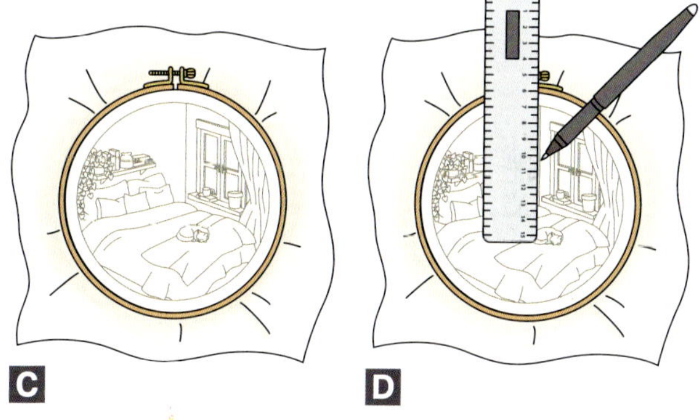

Splitting Thread

1. Cut a length of thread roughly 40˝ (1m) long. Working with a longer piece of thread will lead to more knots.

2. Split the thread into the desired number of strands by gently teasing apart the strands from one end. Hold the split threads in each hand, carefully pulling them apart and allowing the length to untwist itself below your fingers. Pull gently. Set aside the other strands of split thread to use later. **E** **F**

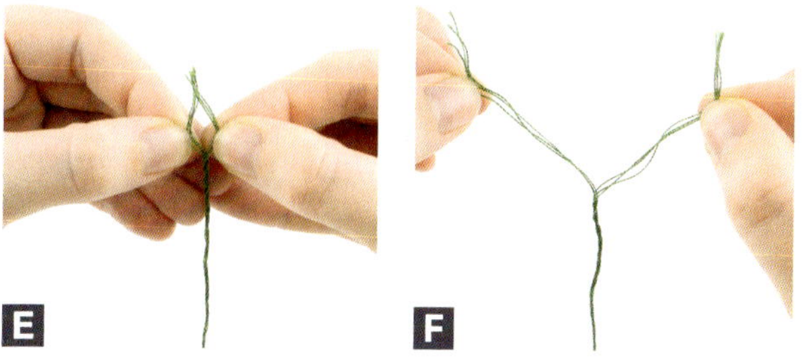

Stitching These Designs

In every project in this book, you will stitch the outlines first, then fill in the colors. You can reverse this order if you prefer, or mix both methods. If you want the outlines to be more prominent, stitch the outlines a second time over the filled-in colors. Filling in the color after stitching the outlines can feel a little like a coloring page or a color-by-number!

Most of the color stitching uses 3 strands of embroidery thread, although there are some exceptions. I sometimes recommend one or two strands for small details, or 6-strands might be suitable to achieve a chunkier look.

Basic Embroidery Stitches

Securing Thread

STARTING

Follow these instructions to knot and prepare the thread before beginning to stitch.

1. Cut a length of thread roughly 40˝ (1m) long, and split it into the required number of strands (see Splitting Thread, page 19). Thread the needle eye, pulling it through a few inches.

2. Wrap the other end of the thread 2–3 times around your index finger, then gently roll the loops off your finger and pull the end tight to create a small knot.

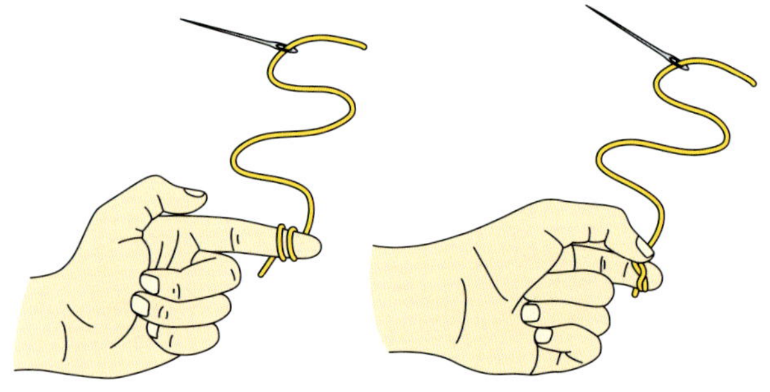

ENDING

When it's time to change colors, or the thread is too short to keep stitching with, finish it securely following this method.

1. Bring the thread to the back of the hoop.

2. At the back of the hoop, tuck the needle under the previous stitch and pull it through. Do this under the same stitch two or three times, so the thread end is secure and won't unravel. Snip away the remaining thread ends.

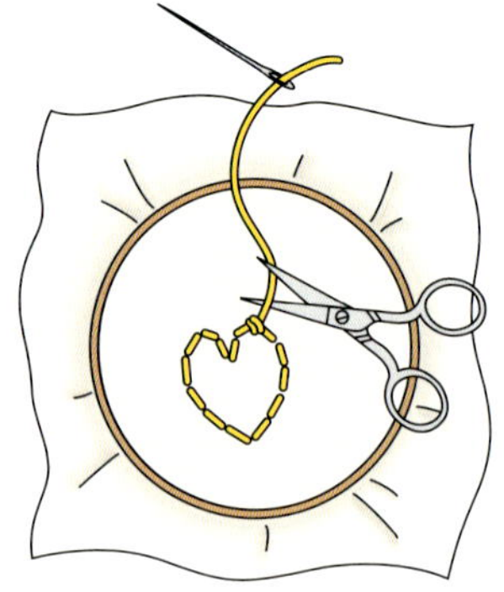

Stitch Library

STRAIGHT STITCH

This basic stitch is the building block for all other stitches. Refer back to this section as needed.

1. Bring the needle up through the fabric at (1), then back down through the fabric at (2), to create a straight stitch. Repeat, varying the length and location for practice.

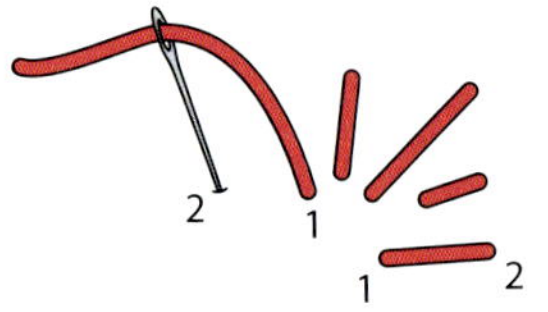

BACKSTITCH

Backstitches are very useful for outlines because they're connected. Make smaller stitches for detailed work, and longer stitches for straight lines.

1. Stitch a straight stitch.

2. Bring the needle up through the fabric ahead of the previous stitch at the distance/length you want the stitch to be (1).

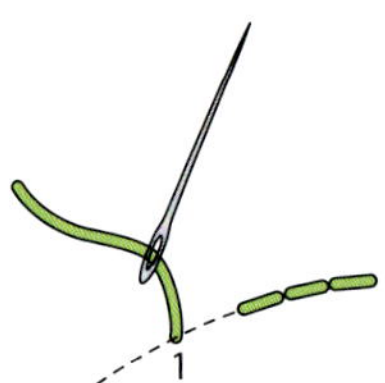

3. Bring the needle down through the fabric right next to, or in the same spot as, where the first stitch ended (2).

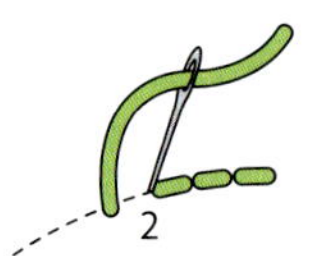

SPLIT STITCH

Split stitches are useful for outlines, or for filling spaces with some textured color. As the name implies, this stitch involves splitting the previous stitch.

1. Stitch a straight stitch.

2. Bring the needle up through the fabric in the middle of the Step 1 stitch, splitting the thread (1).

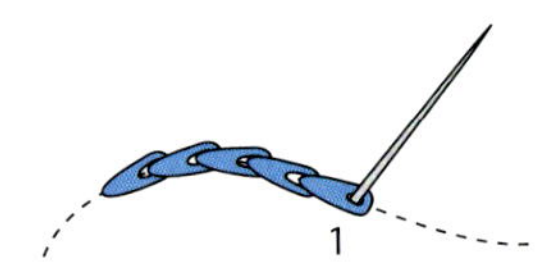

2. Bring the needle down through the fabric at the desired distance to finish the stitch (2).

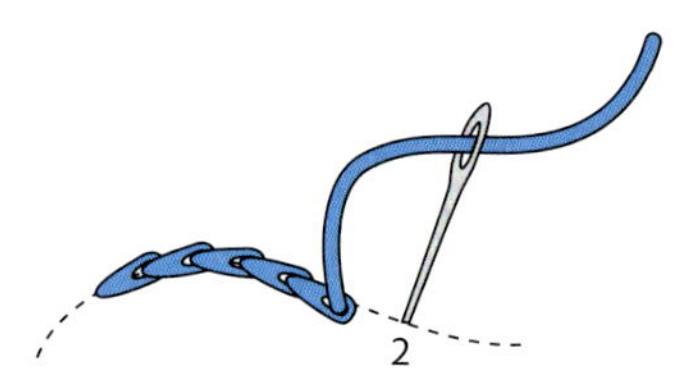

SPLIT BACKSTITCH

Also sometimes called a *reverse split stitch*, a split backstitch combines the two stitches it's named after.

For Line Work

1. Stitch a straight stitch.

2. Bring the needle up through the fabric ahead of the previous stitch at the distance/length you want the stitch to be (1).

3. Bring the needle down through the Step 1 stitch, splitting it (2).

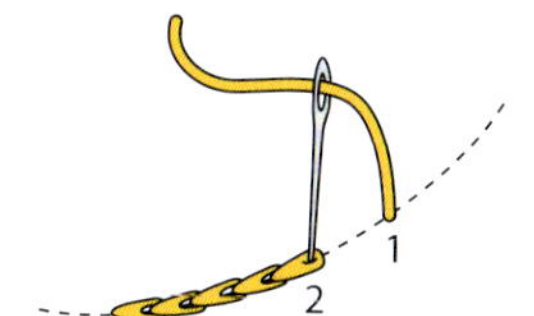

For Fill Work

To fill large spaces with this stitch, work in rows, repeating many lines of stitching (Steps 1–3 above) until the area is filled.

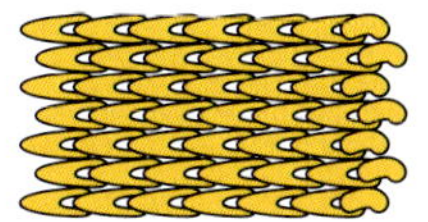

SATIN STITCH

Satin stitch is a filling stitch, meaning it's meant to fill large spaces with smooth color. Pay attention to which direction the satin stitches are running.

1. Bring the needle up through the fabric at one side of the shape to be filled. Stitch a straight stitch that goes all the way to the opposite edge of the shape.

2. Bring the needle up through the fabric as close as possible to the start of the stitch from Step 1 (1). Stitch another straight stitch across the shape, making the two stitches as close together as possible (2). Repeat to fill the entire shape.

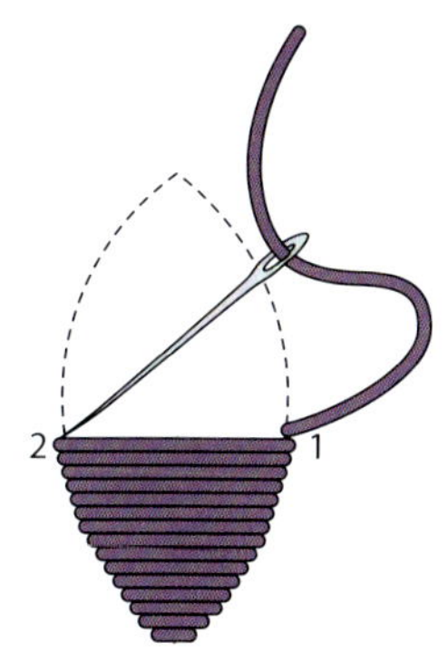

To add dimension when filling asymmetrical shapes, angle the satin stitching. Bring the needle up at the same place as you fill (1), and bring it down further along the shape outline each time (2).

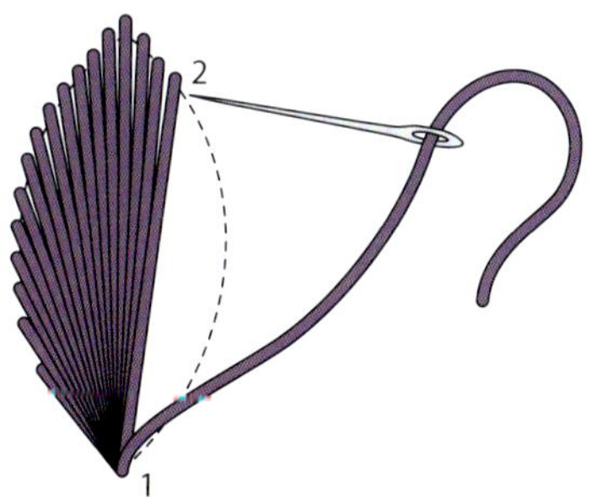

PADDED SATIN STITCH

Padded satin stitches add dimension and depth by layering the thread.

1. Fill the interior of the shape with straight stitches that run perpendicular to the direction that the final satin stitches will go. The stitches do not have to be very neat—just layer several long straight stitches to add bulk.

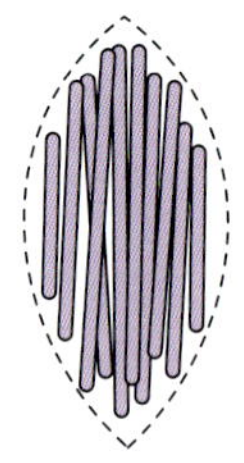

2. Satin stitch (page 23) over top of the Step 1 stitches (perpendicular to them).

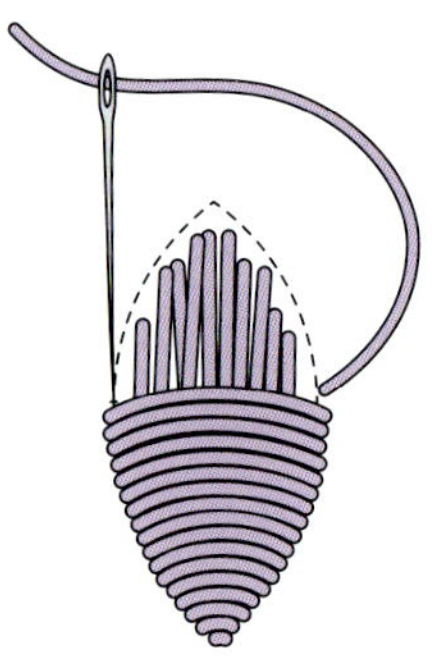

CHAIN STITCH

Chain stitches almost mimic the texture of knitting when done correctly! This gives a lot of texture and character to a home scene.

1. Bring the needle up through the fabric, then down again through the same hole (1). But, don't pull the length of thread all the way through, leaving a loop on top of the hoop (hold with your hand).

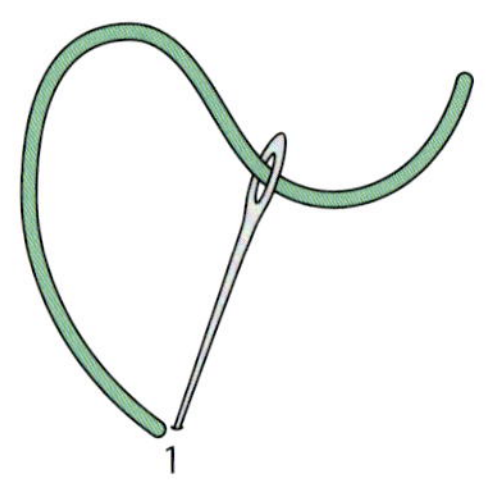

2. Start the next stitch by bringing the needle up through the fabric *inside* of the loop from Step 1 (2). Stitch back down through the fabric in the same spot (3), anchoring the Step 1 loop in place. Be mindful of the tension, as pulling too hard won't result in the right texture.

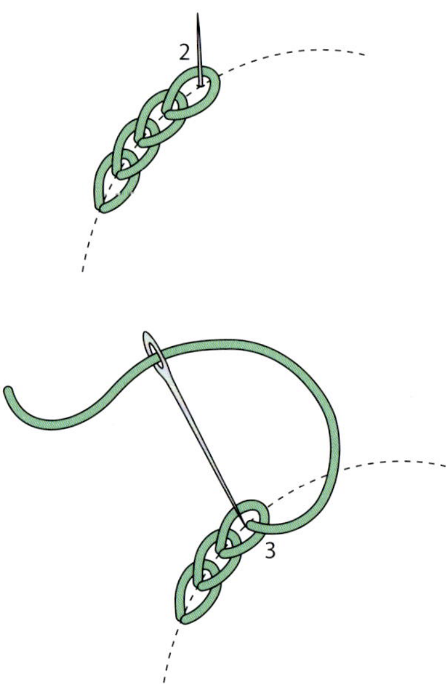

3. To finish, stitch up through the final loop (4), then make a straight stitch over the top edge of the loop (5) to secure it and bring the needle to the back side of the hoop.

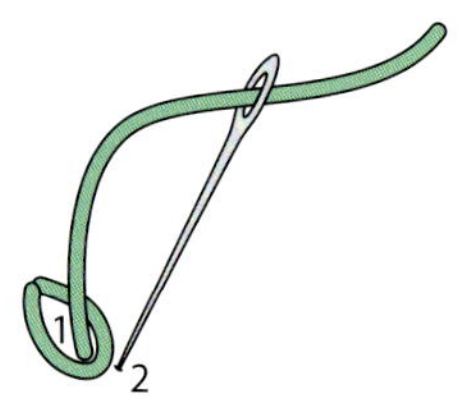

Detached Chain Stitch

A detached chain stitch is a variation sometimes called a *lazy daisy stitch*. It's a simple way to stitch flower petals.

1. Repeat Step 1 in Chain Stitch (left).

2. Bring the needle up through the fabric inside the loop from Step 1, right at the top edge (1). Straight stitch down on the outside of the loop, over the top, to anchor it (2).

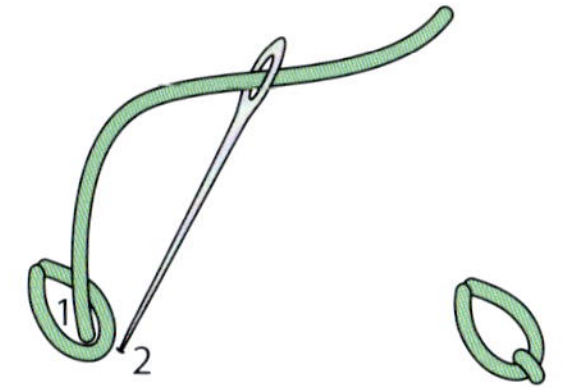

Double Detached Chain Stitch

You can create a smaller detached chain stitch inside of a detached chain stitch to layer the "petals" and create a more detailed flower!

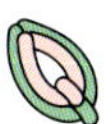

FRENCH KNOTS

French knots can be tricky to master, but they add so much fun texture to a piece! Both hands are needed for this stitch, so try putting the hoop in a hoop frame, or balancing it on a table.

1. Bring the needle up through the fabric (1).

2. Wrap the thread (where it comes out of the fabric) around the needle 2–3 times, wrapping from behind the needle to the front of the needle (2). Keep hold of the thread.

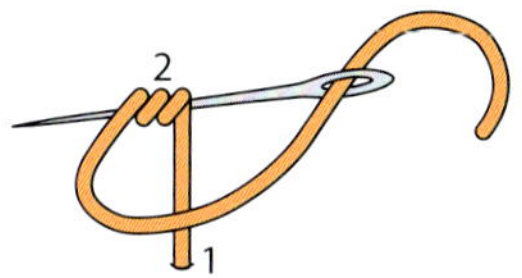

TIP • The more you wrap around the needle, the bigger knot you'll create.

3. Bring the needle back down through the fabric right next to where it came up (3). Gently pull the thread down through the fabric, creating and tightening the knot (4).

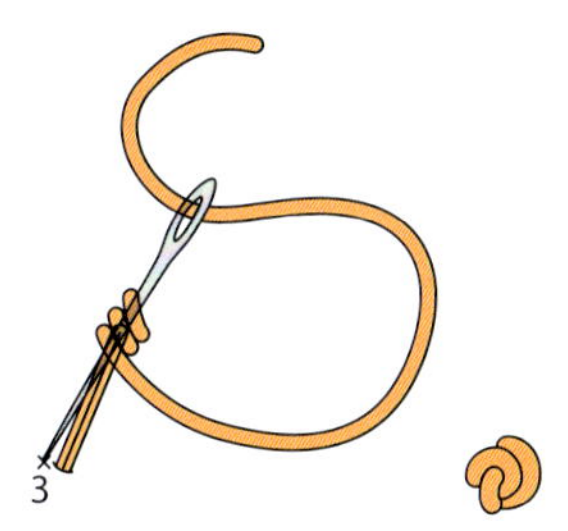

BULLION STITCH

The bullion stitch is similar to a French knot, but because there are more loops over the needle, it is trickier. I recommend practicing on a spare hoop before trying this stitch on a final embroidery.

1. Bring the needle up through the fabric (1) and make a backstitch (page 22) the desired length of the bullion knot (2, 3). Do not pull the needle and thread all the way through.

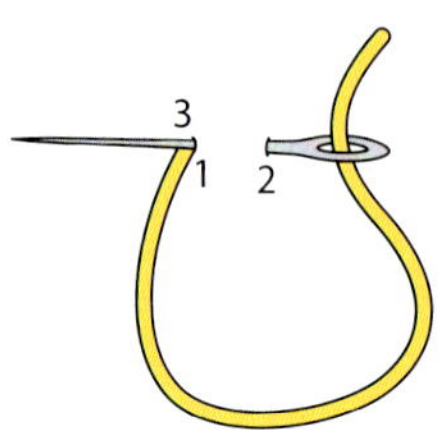

2. Wrap the thread around the needle until the wraps are the same length as the Step 1 backstitch (4). More wraps will create a longer bullion stitch. Carefully angle the needle to compare the wrapped thread to the stitch.

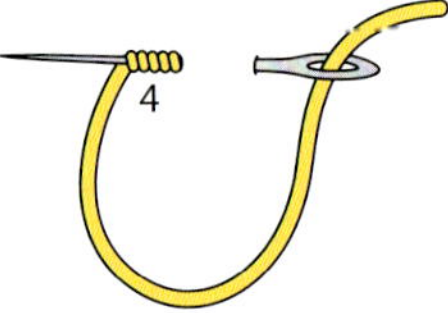

3. Carefully pull the needle tip forward through the wraps. As you pull the needle, the knot will form (5). Bring the needle back into the fabric at the end of the knot (6).

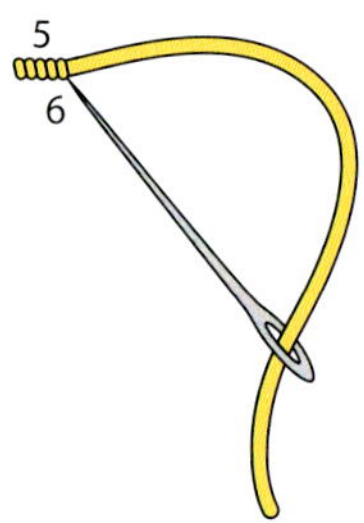

Looped Bullion Stitch

Looping bullion stitches is a great way to stitch funky and 3D flowers.

1. Make a very small backstitch (page 22). Repeat Step 2 in Bullion Stitch (left) to wrap the thread around the needle. Wrap double the amount of loops when compared to the standard bullion stitch.

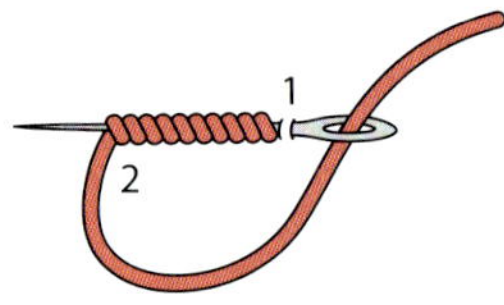

2. Pull the tip of the needle through as with the standard bullion stitch. The dense wrapping will naturally curl the bullion stitch into a loop. Bring the needle back down through the fabric at the base of the loop (3).

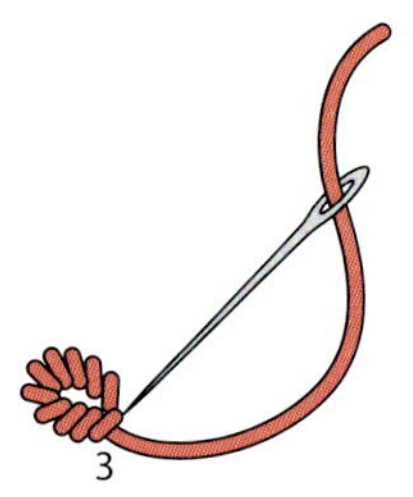

TURKEYWORK

Turkeywork texture is perfect for depicting tassels or blanket trims.

1. Bring the needle up through the fabric, and then back down through the fabric right next to where it emerged (1). Do not pull the thread all the way through, leaving a loop. Use a finger to hold the loop in place if needed.

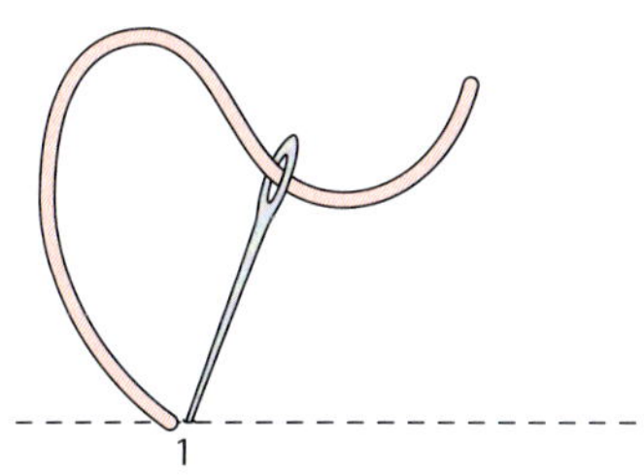

2. Anchor the loop by stitching a small straight stitch at the base of the loop, overlapping the two threads of the loop (2, 3).

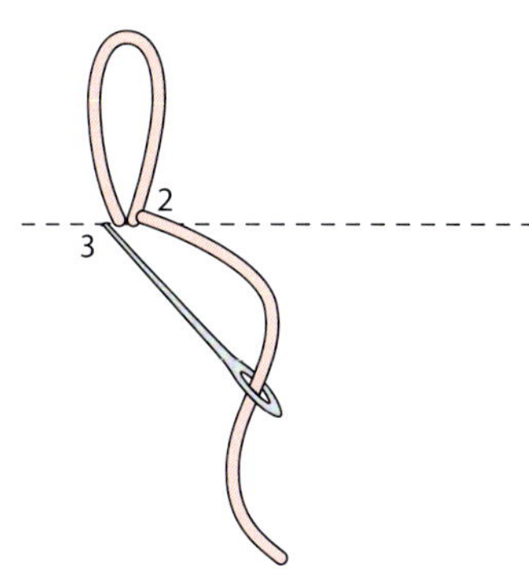

3. Repeat Steps 1–2, making rows of loops, or filling an area with a row of loops (4). Use a pair of scissors to cut the tops of the loops (5), then trim the strands to the desired length. Trimming the strands short will create a fur-like texture, while leaving them longer will look more fluffy.

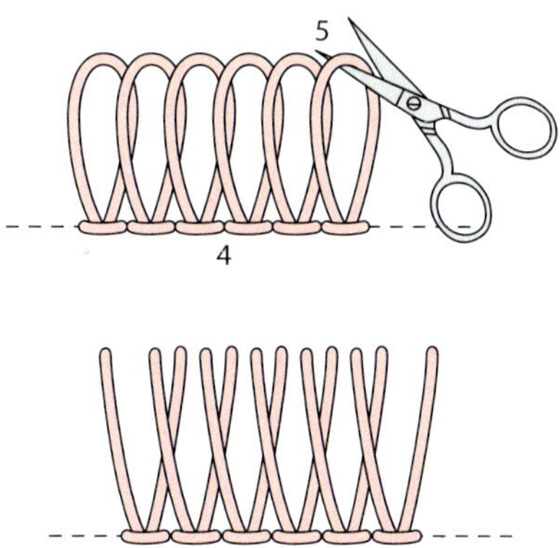

TIP • Once the loops are all cut and trimmed, fluff the strands up with a finger. This will separate the strands of the thread and create a fluffier feel.

Tassels

1. Repeat Steps 1–2 in Turkeywork (left) to stitch 3–4 loops in a group, as close to one another as possible (1). Anchor all of the loops with one straight securing stitch at the base (2).

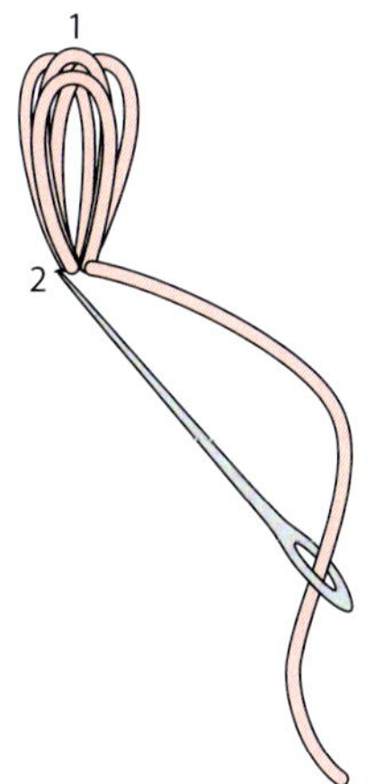

2. Trim and fluff up the threads (3).

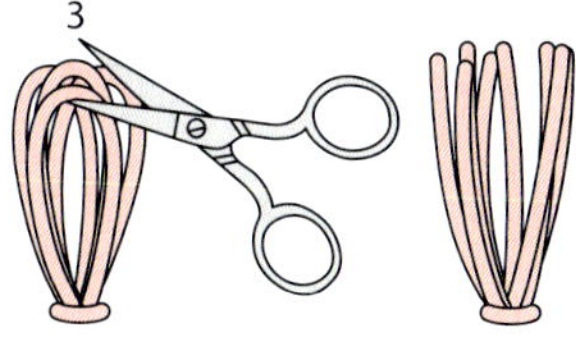

COUCHING STITCHES

Couching stitches are a simple way to hold thread and objects in place on a hoop.

1. Place and arrange the object or yarn on the hoop that you want to stitch down (blue yarn illustrated).

2. At even intervals along the length (roughly ½″, or closer together if the yarn is curved) of the yarn, straight stitch (page 22) over the yarn with the embroidery thread (orange thread illustrated). Bring the needle up and down very close together (1, 2).

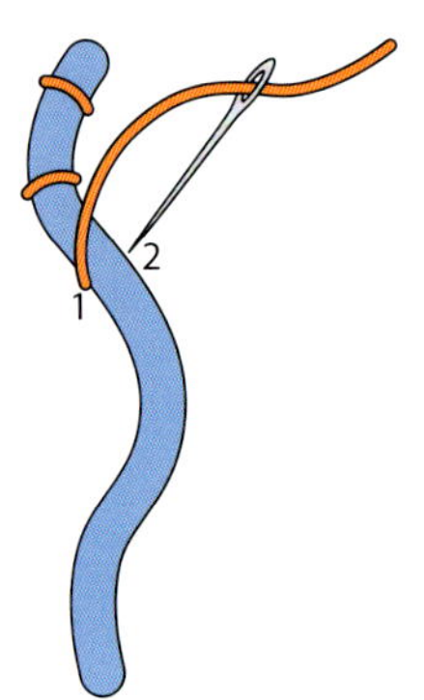

MORE USES • You can also use couching stitches over previously stitched areas to add texture. The couching stitches don't always have to go in and out of the fabric in the same place.

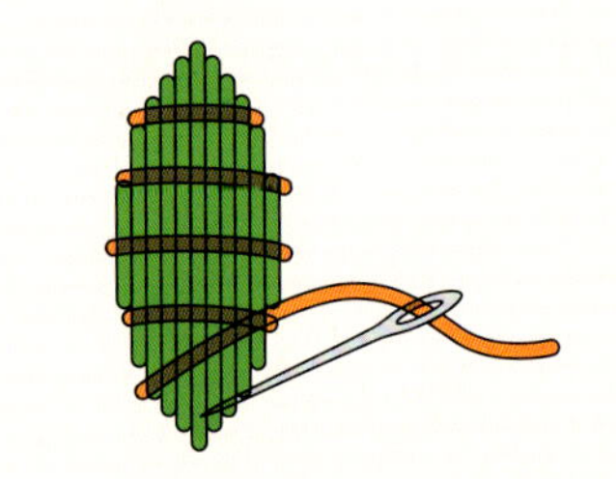

Use couching stitches to attach an object. Follow the same steps, making sure to account for the shape and weight of the object.

WEAVING STITCHES

Basic Weave Stitch

Weave stitch, or basketweave stitch, involves stitching a foundation of parallel stitches, then literally weaving a second set of stitches over and under the foundation. It creates a beautiful textured, woven look, and is also a lot of fun to stitch!

1. Stitch parallel, vertical straight stitches with a 1mm gap between the stitches. If you want to make a tighter woven area, make the stitches closer, or for a looser woven area, make the stitches further apart.

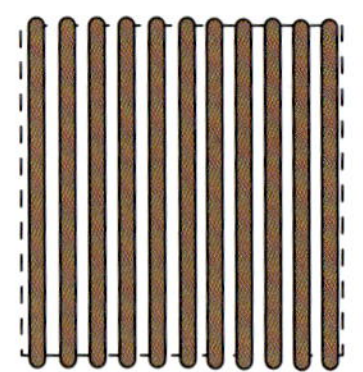

2. Bring the needle up through the fabric at one corner (1). Weave the needle over and under (alternating) the vertical stitches from Step 1 (2). Pull the thread flat with the bottom of the shape, then bring the needle down through the fabric in the opposite corner.

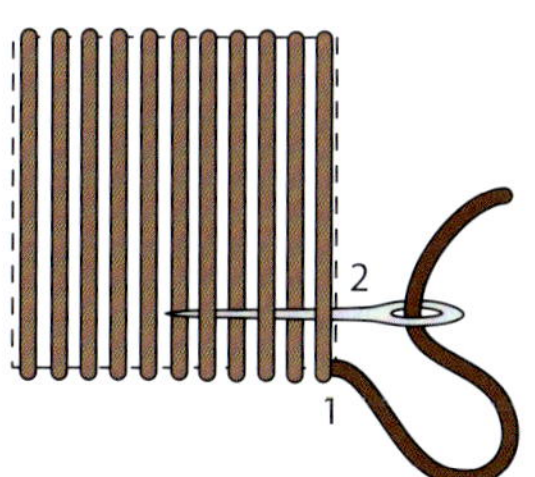

3. Repeat Step 2, bringing the needle up through the fabric just above the previous row. Weave opposite the previous row, then stitch down through the fabric on the opposite side (3). Repeat until the shape is filled (4).

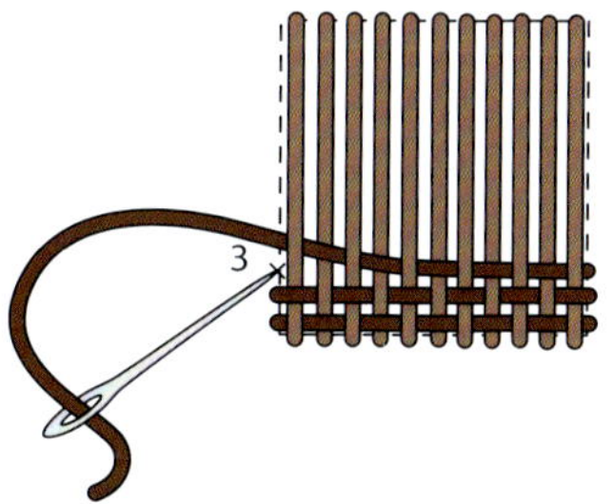

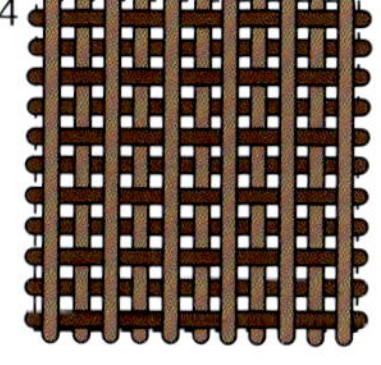

TIP • Use the needle to adjust the horizontal rows. Try to make them lie straight and flat before starting the next row.

Ribbed Weave Stitch

This is a weave stitch variation which creates a cool ribbed texture! Be careful not to pull the thread too hard; instead let the thread form loops along the row.

1. Stitch vertical straight lengths across the space to be filled about 5mm apart.

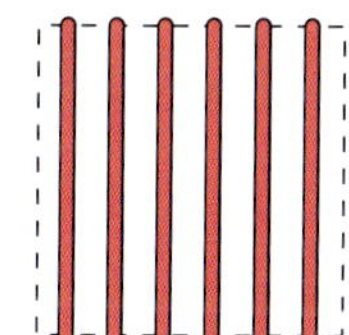

2. Bring the needle up through the fabric at the top right corner of the shape (1). Weave the needle under the first vertical length (2).

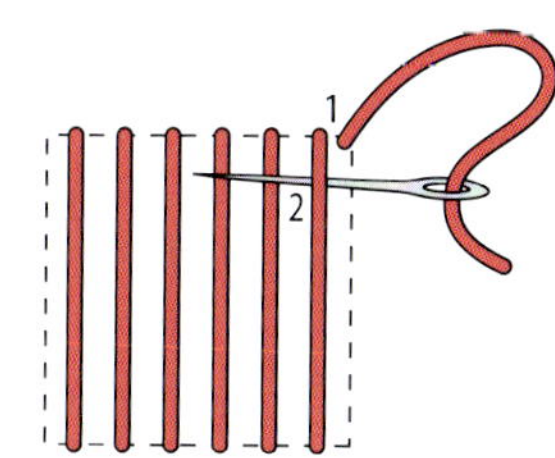

3. Bring the needle back in front of the first vertical length (3), then weave the needle under the first and second vertical lengths together (4).

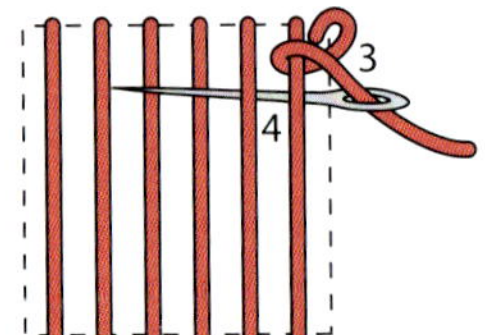

4. Bring the needle back in front of the second vertical length, then weave the needle under the second and third vertical length. Continue this pattern of weaving to the end of the row, looping around each stitch then going under two stitches.

Stitch back down through the fabric at the end of the row (5). Don't pull too hard on the thread. Use your finger to push the loops to the top of the shape.

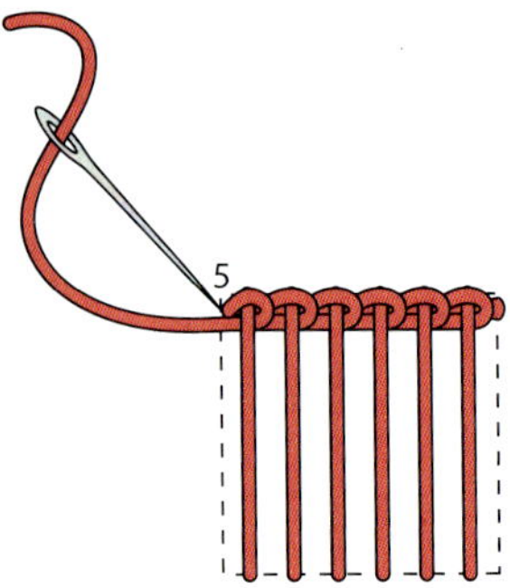

5. For the next row, bring the needle up at the right side, below the first row. Always work rows right to left. Repeat Steps 2–5 to fill the space with rows of ribbed weave stitch.

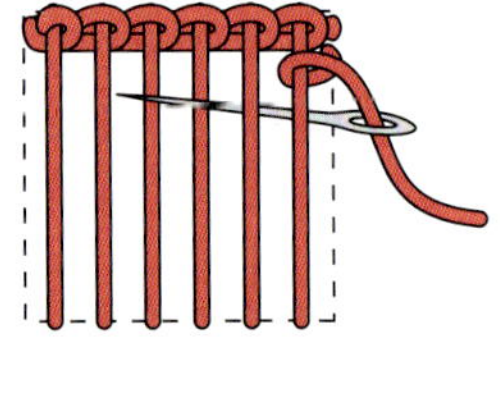

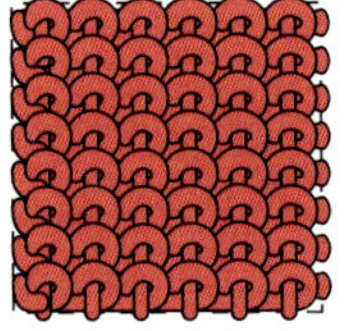

Woven Wheel

This is a really beautiful stitch for roses. It's also really fun to make!

1. Stitch 5 straight stitches like the spokes of a wheel within a circle. For bigger flowers, use more spokes! Always use an odd number of spokes.

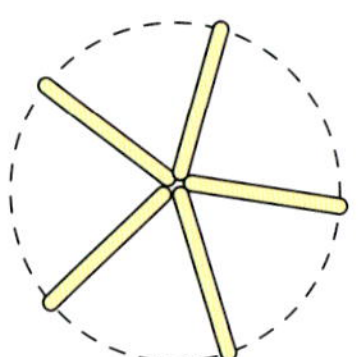

2. Bring the needle up through the fabric in the center. Start weaving over and under the stitches from Step 1 in a spiral. As the thread weaves around, the layers will build up and resemble the layered petals of a rose. Use your finger to adjust the strands if needed.

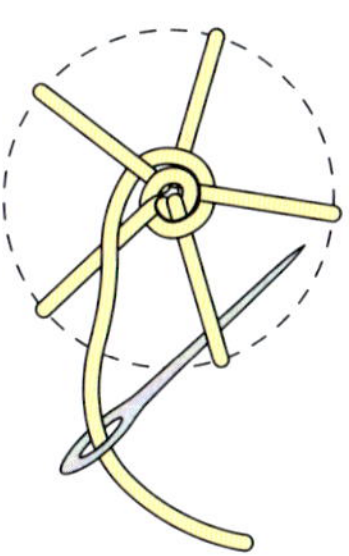

TIP • When weaving the thread round and round, it might be easier to also turn the hoop in your hands to have the best angle for each spoke.

3. Once the straight stitches are completely covered, bring the needle back through the fabric at the edge of the circle.

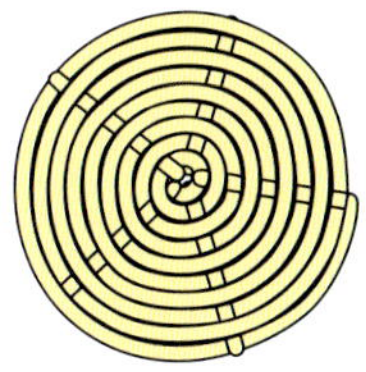

Woven Trellis

This woven technique creates three dimensional triangles—perfect for stitching leaves! It is sometimes called *picot stitch*.

1. Add a pin at the desired tip of the triangle. Bring the needle up through the fabric at the desired location of the triangle base (1), bring the thread over the pin (2), and then bring the needle back down through the fabric at the other side of the triangle base (3).

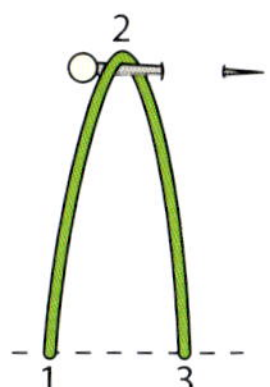

2. Bring the needle up through the fabric in the center of the triangle base (4), wrap the thread around the pin (5), then begin to weave over and under the three vertical stitches from top to bottom (6). Alternate the over and under in each row, working left to right, then right to left. Keep your tension loose, and use the needle to adjust the rows.

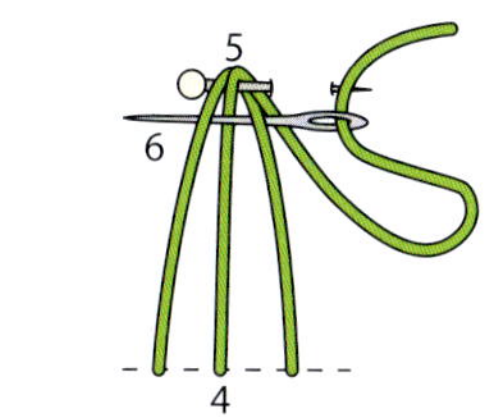

3. Once the entire framework is covered, bring the needle back through the fabric on one side (8), and carefully remove the pin. The leaf will now be three dimensional!

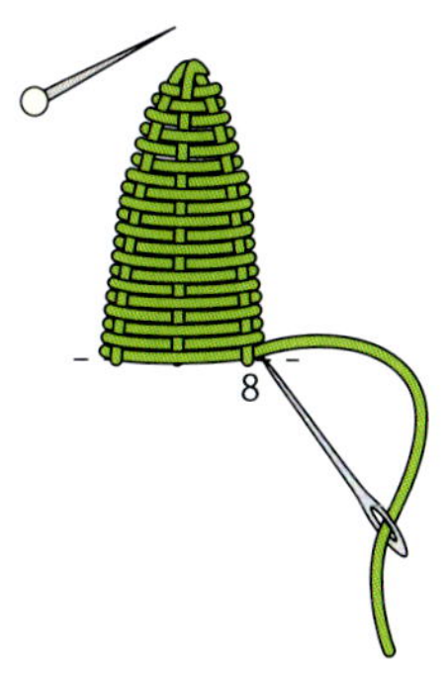

Ceylon Stitch

This stitch creates an amazing knit texture, but it is challenging. The most important thing is to keep even tension.

1. Stitch a line of backstitches (page 22) at the top and bottom of the shape to be filled. The length of the backstitches will determine if the ceylon stitch is tight (short backstitches) or loose (long backstitches). It can be more difficult to ceylon stitch with short backstitches.

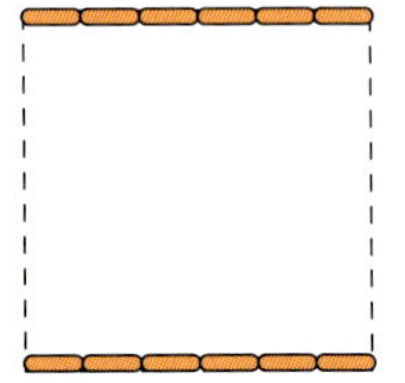

2. To create the first row of loops, bring the needle up a little way down the shape from the top left corner (1). Bring the needle through the first backstitch, from the top down (2), and over the thread (3). Repeat along the whole row of backstitches. At the end of the row, bring the needle back through the fabric on the right side.

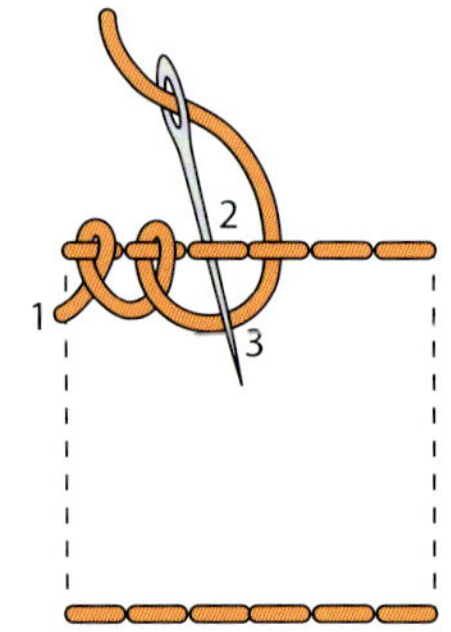

3. For the next row, again bring the needle up a little way down the shape on the left (4). Bring the needle through the loop above it (the previous row), as seen in the illustration (5). Repeat for the entire row, and repeat the rows from left to right to fill the shape.

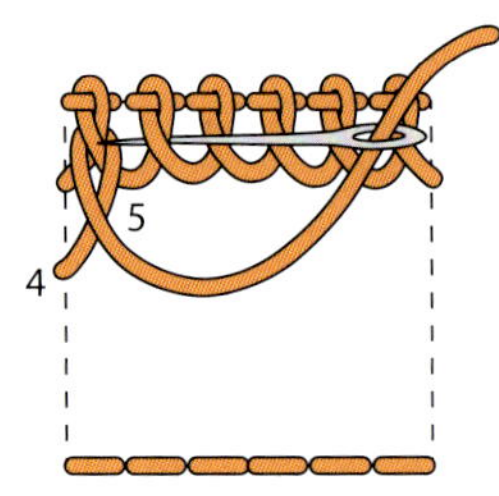

4. For the final row, bring the needle through the above loops like before (6), and then anchor it to the bottom row of backstitch by bringing the needle under the backstitch from the top down (7). Complete the whole row and then bring the needle back through the fabric at the bottom right corner.

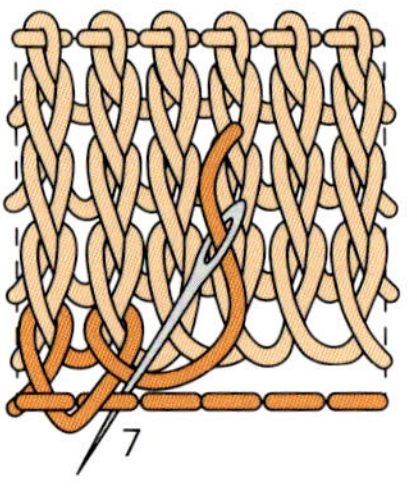

LONG AND SHORT STITCH

Also called *thread painting*, long and short stitch is a technique for stitching more realistic subjects by blending colors together. The more layers and gradients of a color you use, the more realistic the embroidery will become!

1. At the top of the shape, stitch alternating long and short straight stitches using the darkest value thread. If using three shades, make the long stitches come down a third of the shape. Adjust the size of each color area based on the number of colors you're using. It might be helpful to draw guidelines.

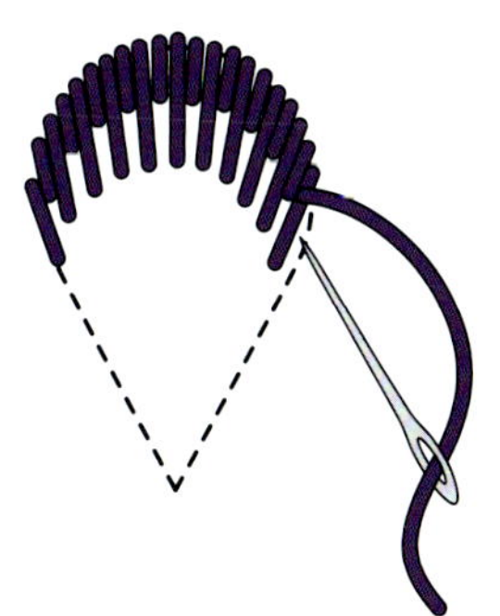

2. Using the medium value thread, fill the middle third of the shape with another layer of long and short stitches. Match the stitches with the stitching from Step 1 (long stitches in Step 1 meet short stitches in this step, and vice versa). If you're filling an irregular shape, angle the stitches to reflect the shape.

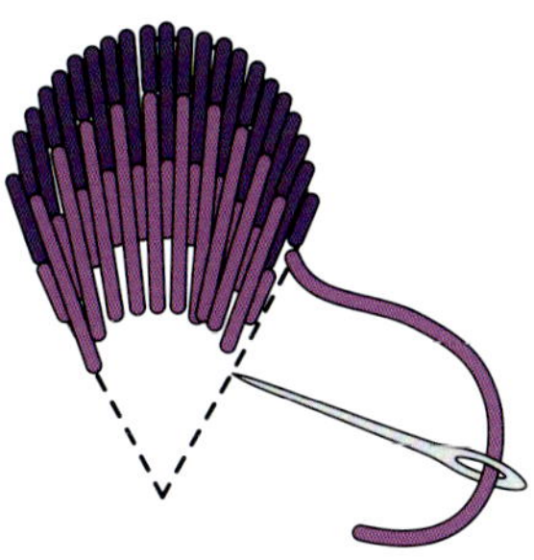

3. Fill the final third of the shape with the lightest value, again using long and short stitches.

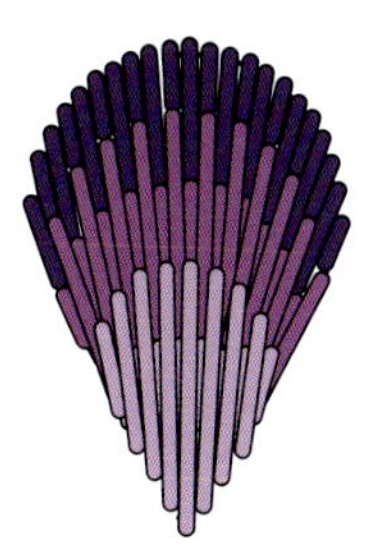

BEADING

Adding beads to an embroidery is fun, textural, and interesting. Always add beads last to avoid snagging threads on the beads. You may need a thinner beading needle depending on the size of the beads. Likewise, use only 1 or 2 strands of thread.

Single Beads

1. Bring the needle up through the fabric (1), and thread the bead onto the needle (2).

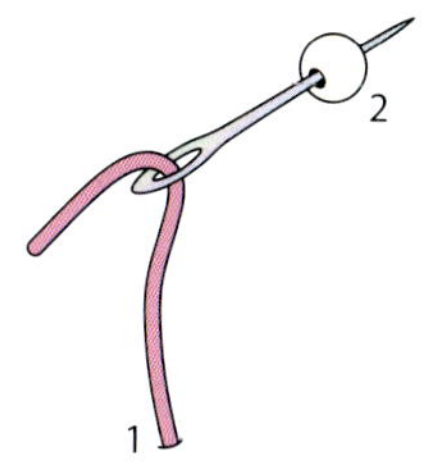

2. Slide the bead to the base of the thread (where it meets the fabric), then bring the needle down right next to the bead (3).

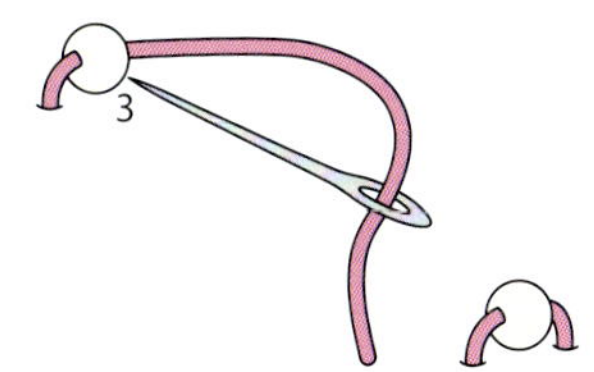

Beads with Sequins

1. Bring the needle up through the fabric (1). Thread a sequin onto the needle (2), and then thread a bead (3).

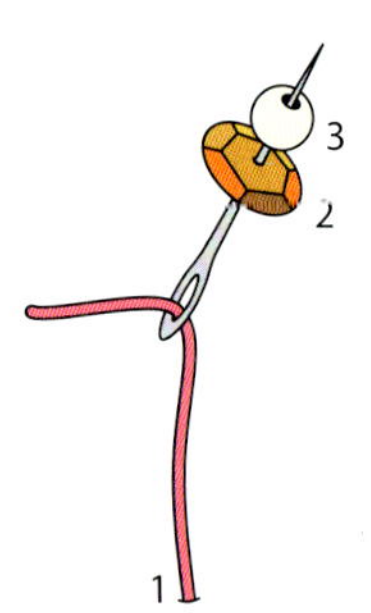

2. Thread the sequin down to the base of the thread (where it meets the fabric). Bring the needle back through both the sequin and the fabric (4), moving the bead so it sits on top of the sequin.

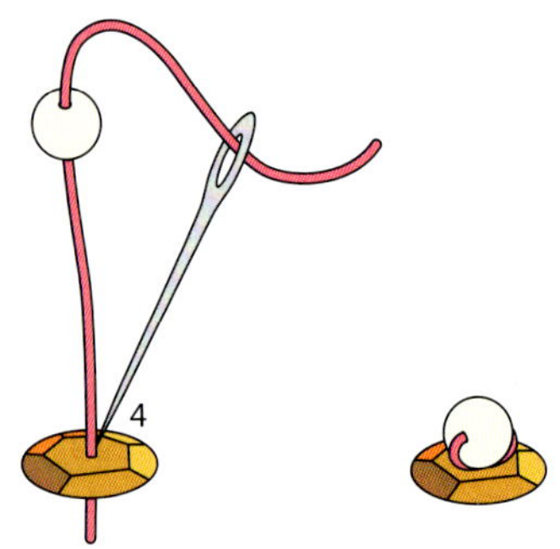

Bead Rows

1. Bring the needle up through the fabric (1), and thread all the desired beads for one row onto the needle (2).

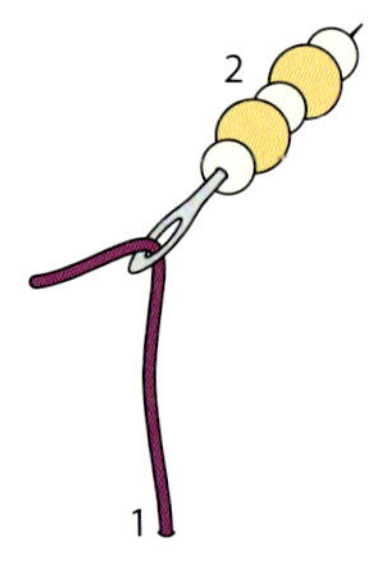

2. Bring the needle down through the fabric on the other side of the bead row (3). Then, bring the needle up and down between each bead, couching over the thread between each bead (see Couching Stitch page 28), anchoring the row to the fabric (4, 5).

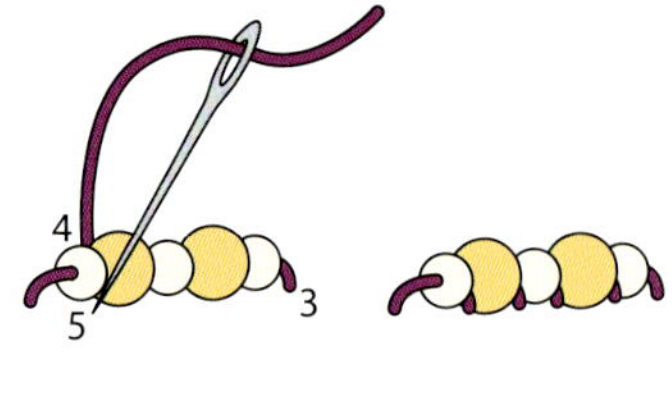

FINISHING STITCHES

These stitches can be used in the actual embroidery, but they are also very helpful for finishing and neatening the back of the hoop.

Running Stitch

Running stitch is so simple! Use this for gathering the excess 'skirt' of fabric around the hoop.

1. Bring the needle up through the fabric, and make a straight stitch (1, 2).

2. Repeat Step 1, stitching a line with gaps between each stitch (3, 4). After creating a row of stitches, you can pull on the thread to gather the fabric. Longer stitches makes gathering easier.

Once you're used to running stitch, try gathering more stitches on the needle before pulling the needle through to make the process faster.

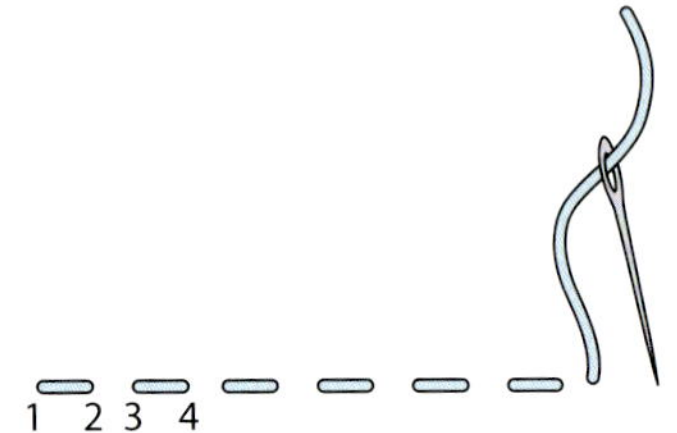

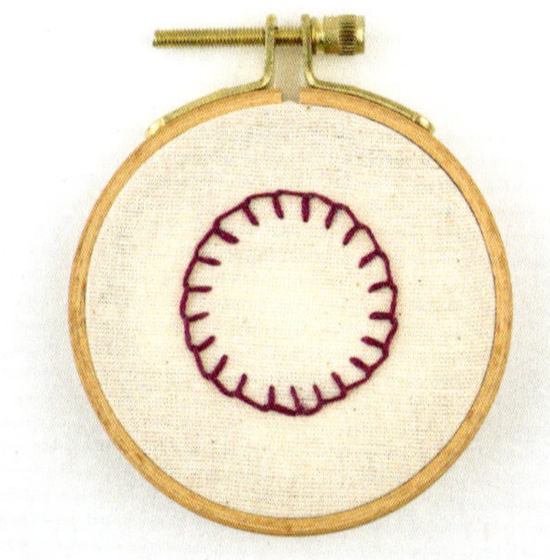

Blanket Stitch

The lovely blanket stitch is great for covering the edges of fabric.

1. Bring the needle up through the fabric just inside the edge of the stitch line (1).

2. Make a stitch through the fabric from inside the edge (2) to the edge (3). As you pull the needle through, catch the thread on the stitch (4). Repeat, keeping the space between stitches even.

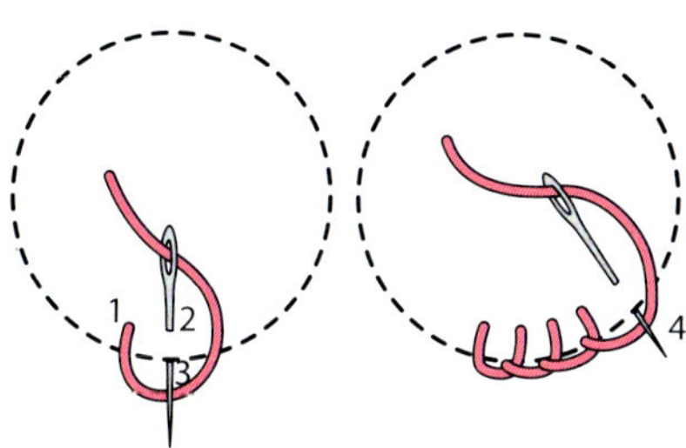

3. If stitching a circle, join the beginning and end with a horizontal straight stitch into the first stitch (5).

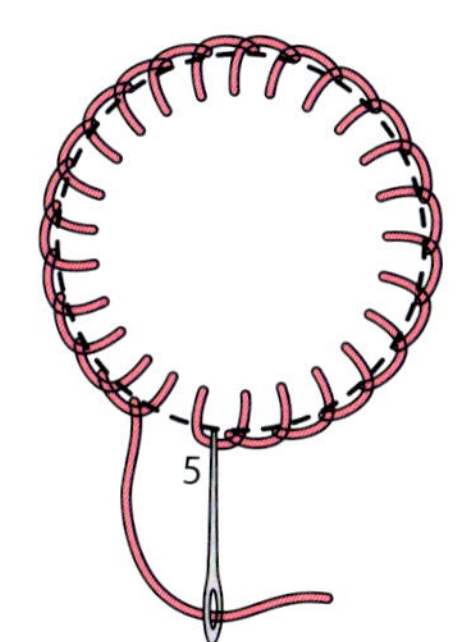

In a Knot?

Knots happen to the best of us, for a variety of reasons. The main rule is not to panic!

When the thread knots, fight the impulse to tug frantically because you might make the knot even tighter. Gently pull on different strands in the knot, using your fingers or your needle. Most of the time, this will loosen it enough to unravel easily. If the knot has a big loop coming out of it, hold the thread and pull at the loop gently.

Some knots are here to stay. If an impossible knot happens at the back of the fabric, it's no big deal since the back is meant to be messy! Cut the thread and start again from where you left off. Likewise, if the knot happens at the front, neatly snip off the thread at the fabric, and start again from where you cut.

Embroidery thread has a habit of twisting up as you stitch. To prevent knots, un-twist the thread in the opposite direction when you notice it twisting by rolling the needle between your finger and thumb.

Display and Finishing

It's important to decide ahead of time how you want to display your embroidery once it's finished, as it will affect the stitching process. The projects in this book use the seal-in-the-hoop method (right) because it's the best way to give whole hoop embroideries perfect tension. However, this isn't the only option.

You can display your projects in the embroidery hoop, or get a special circular embroidery hoop frame. You could paint and decorate your hoop to add interest, or transfer it into a rubber wood-effect hoop (see Hoops, page 8). You can hang it up with a beautiful ribbon or add a hanging tassel at the bottom. Alternatively, frame the embroidery in a square frame, with a custom circular mat. You could even expand the pattern and crop the edges square, perfect for framing.

Seal-In-The-Hoop Method

Seal-in-the-hoop is for full-hoop circular embroideries. This method is a life-saver for keeping the tension even all the way around. Keep in mind this method involves stitching the inner hoop into the embroidery, so it cannot be removed from the hoop afterward.

1. Load the fabric into the hoop with the design facing right side up (see Transfer Methods, page 18). If using wash-away transfer paper, stitch the outline first, and then wash the paper away.

2. Cut the fabric outside of the hoop, leaving a 1″ (2.5 cm) 'skirt' of excess fabric around the hoop. **A**

A

3. Using 1 strand of black pearl thread, re-stitch the outer circle of the design with split backstitch (page 23) (from the front of the hoop). Stitch through both the fabric inside the hoop and the excess skirt behind it. Ensure that the excess fabric is tightly secured down. **B**

4. Continue to stitch in the hoop, overlapping the skirt on the backside whenever necessary. **C**

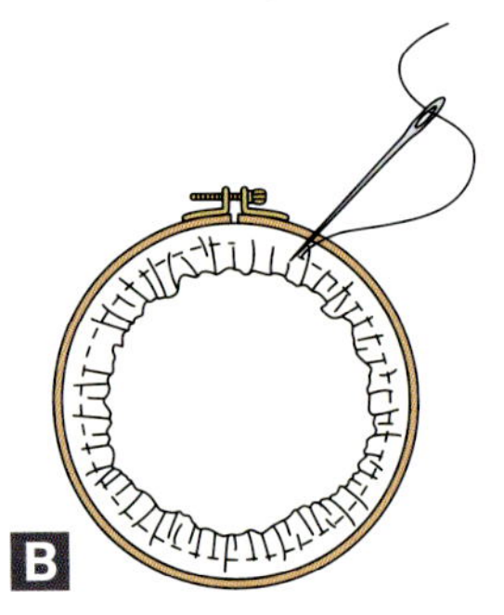

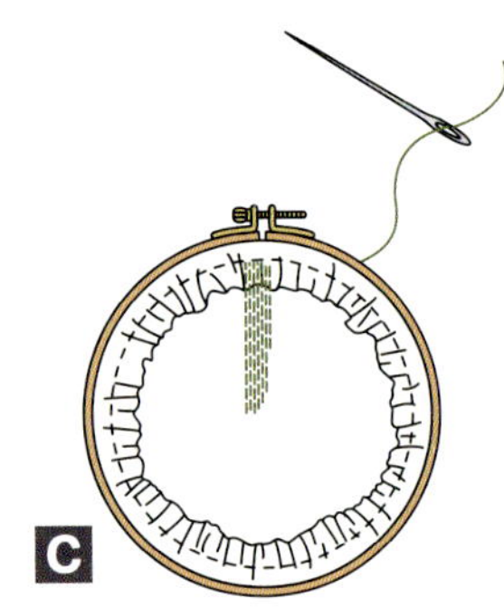

Gathering Edges Method

The gathering method is for finishing a hoop after the embroidery is complete.

1. Cut the fabric outside of the hoop, leaving a 1˝ (2.5 cm) 'skirt' of excess fabric around the hoop. **D**

2. Stitch a line of running stitches (page 34) around the edge of the skirt, ½˝ (1.3cm) from the edge. Keep the stitches loose and fairly long, about ⅜˝ (1 cm) each. **E**

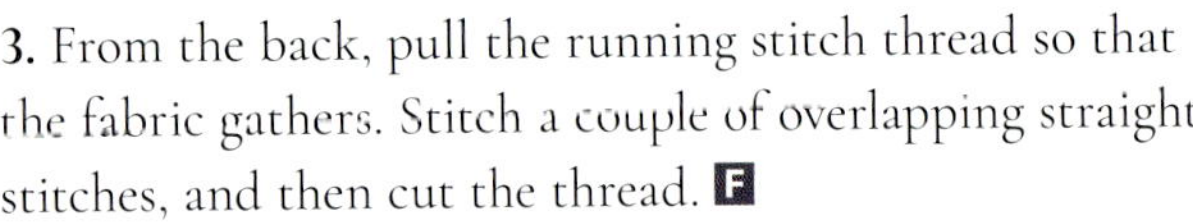

3. From the back, pull the running stitch thread so that the fabric gathers. Stitch a couple of overlapping straight stitches, and then cut the thread. **F**

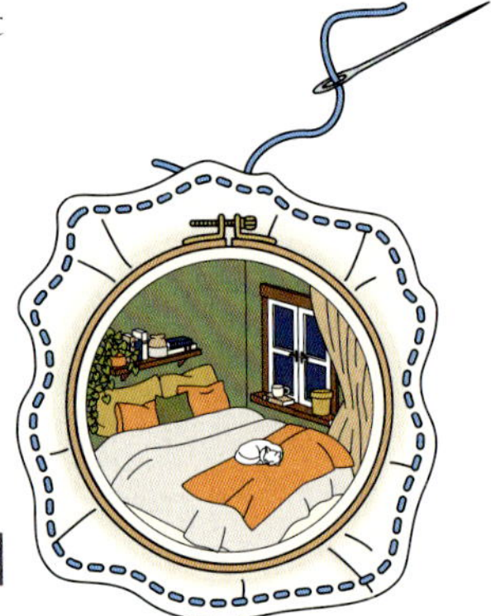

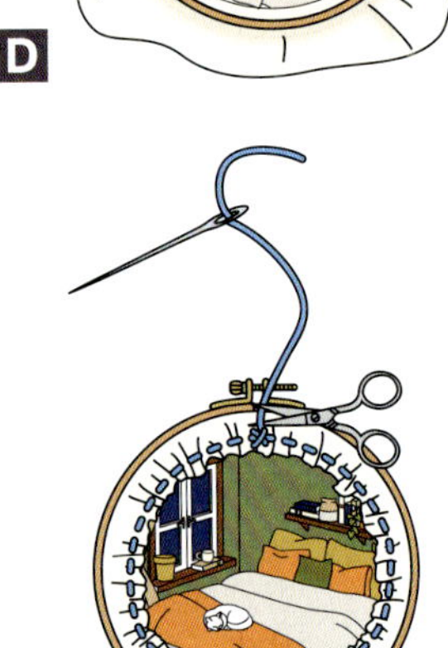

Backing (Optional)

If you want to cover the gathered fabric edges and the messy back of the stitching, add a backing. Felt is a good option because it doesn't fray.

1. Cut a circle of felt, slightly smaller than the size of the hoop. **G**

2. Stitch (or blanket stitch) it to the gathered skirt fabric. Stitch through both the felt and the fabric. **H**

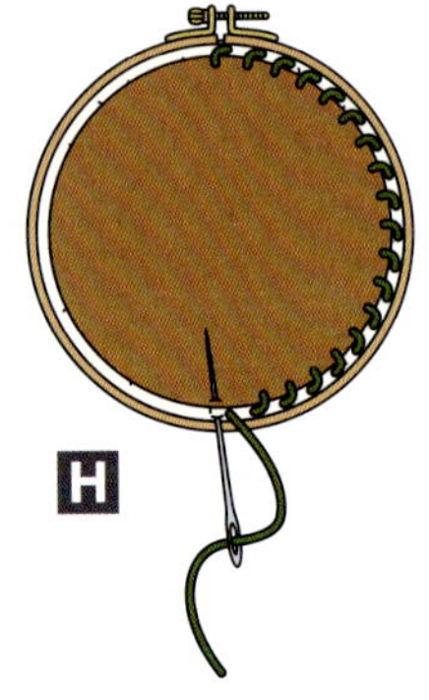

Other Finishing Methods

You can research lots of methods for finishing, but here are a few more ideas.

- Cut a circle of cardboard (or even thin wood) exactly the same size as the inner hoop. Press the circle to the back of the hoop, over the fabric skirt, and it should hold securely and snugly.
- Cut the excess fabric skirt into tabs, and glue the tabs to the inner hoop circle. If you want to add a backing, glue a circle of fabric over the stitching. Make sure to use textile safe glue that won't degrade the piece.
- Decide not to back the hoop and display the messy, fascinating back with pride in a frame or hoop!

PROJECTS

Color Guides

Every project includes comprehensive DMC color code references called color guides. The color guides indicate exactly which color is used in each section of the design. For more intricate projects, magnified color guides are also provided. Feel free to customize each project with your preferred colors or use these guides as a reference when selecting alternatives from different brands.

Stitch Direction Guides

Additionally, each project has stitch direction guides that indicate which direction your stitches should flow. For example, horizontal arrows across a shape indicate that the stitching should be horizontal in that area. Stitch direction has a big impact on the realism and dimensionality of your finished piece. These directional guides apply to various techniques, including split backstitch and satin stitch, offering helpful suggestions while leaving room for your personal stitching preferences. If it helps, copy the direction lines onto your pattern with an erasable pen to guide the stitching.

Templates

To access the templates as a downloadable PDF, scan this QR code or go to tinyurl.com/11616-patterns-download

Finished size: 8″ hoop

Woven Living Room

This calm, organic living room design uses weave stitch and a neutral color palette to create a cozy and homey space. The 3D wall hanging adds dimension and texture to the classic scene.

TOOLS & MATERIALS

11½″ × 11½″ (29cm × 29cm) lightweight cotton linen fabric in a light neutral color

8″ (20cm) wooden embroidery hoop

2 embroidery needles (size 5)

Tapestry needle (size 22)

2¾″ × 4″ (7cm × 10cm) rectangle of cardboard

2″ (5cm) long wooden dowel (4mm thick)

Ruler

Pencil

Paper scissors

Tape

Fineline pen

Woven Living Room Template (page 40)

THREAD

1 ball DMC pearl cotton, 310 (size 12)

1 ball DMC pearl cotton, BLANC (size 12)

DMC 6-strand embroidery floss

- 937 (sage green)—1 skein
- 437 (pale brown)—1 skein
- 739 (pale yellow)—1 skein
- 712 (pale cream/pink)—4 skeins
- 3864 (dusty pink)—1 skein
- BLANC (white)—1 skein
- 543 (pale dusty pink)—2 skeins
- 890 (dark green)—1 skein
- 435 (brown)—1 skein
- 738 (dusty yellow)—1 skein

Wool (for mini wall hanging)

- DMC tapestry wool yarn, BLANC (white)—1 skein
- DMC Eco Vita organic wool yarn, 203 (mustard)—1 skein
- DMC Eco Vita organic wool yarn, 002 (beige)—1 skein

STITCHES USED

Split Backstitch (page 23)

Satin Stitch (page 23)

Basic Weave Stitch (page 28)

Ribbed Weave Stitch (page 29)

Woven Wheel (page 30)

Ceylon Stitch (page 32)

design anthology UK
ISSUE 19
design anthology UK
ISSUE 14

Outline

1. Load the fabric onto the hoop, and tighten the screw so the fabric tension is like the surface of a drum (see Prepare the Hoop, page 16).

2. Transfer the design onto the fabric (see Transfer Methods, page 18). I use the wash-away transfer paper method. **A**

3. Stitch all the outlines in split backstitch with 1 strand of 310 pearl thread. **B**

4. If you're using dissolvable transfer paper, remove the fabric from the hoop, and wash away the paper. Wait for the fabric to fully dry, iron it flat, then load the fabric back into the hoop. As you tighten, make sure that the straight lines of stitching are still straight.

5. Optional: If you plan to finish the project using the seal-in-the-hoop method (page 36), trim the outer skirt of fabric to 1" (2.5cm). Then, using 1 strand of the 310 pearl thread, stitch around the outline circle with split backstitch, stitching through the fabric skirt. **C**

A

B

C

Color guide

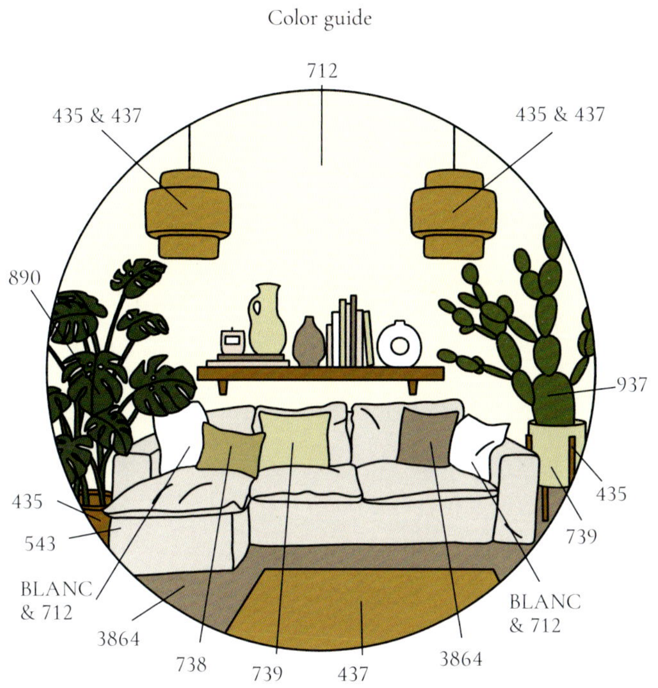

Detail color guide

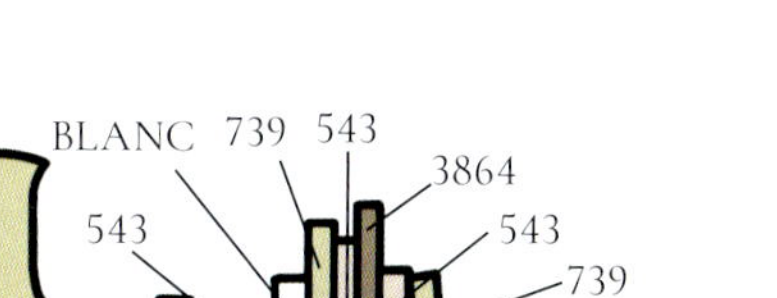

Fill Color

Unless otherwise stated, use 3 strands of embroidery floss to fill the color. Stay inside the stitched outlines. Refer to the color guides at the beginning of the project and stitch direction guides in each section as needed.

CACTUS

Fill the cactus with 937 and satin stitch, following the direction of the cactus segments as shown. Stitch horizontal rows of split backstitch to fill the cactus pot with 739. Stitch vertical rows of split backstitch to fill the pot legs with 435. **D**

MONSTERA

1. Fill the monstera plant with 890. Use split backstitch to fill the stems and satin stitch to fill the leaves. Angle the satin stitches to fill the curved shapes. Instead of keeping the satin stitches parallel to each other, bring the needle up close together, then angle them outward to fill the shape. **E**

2. Using horizontal rows of split backstitch, fill the monstera plant pot with 435. Use tiny satin stitches to fill the pot rim with the same color. **F**

E

F

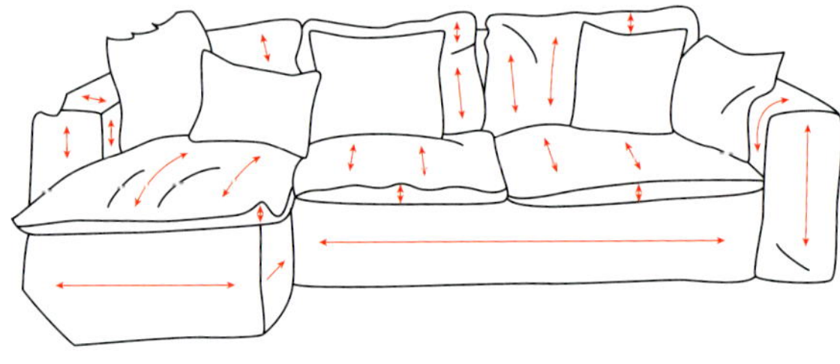

G

SOFA

Fill the sofa with rows of split backstitch in 543. **G**

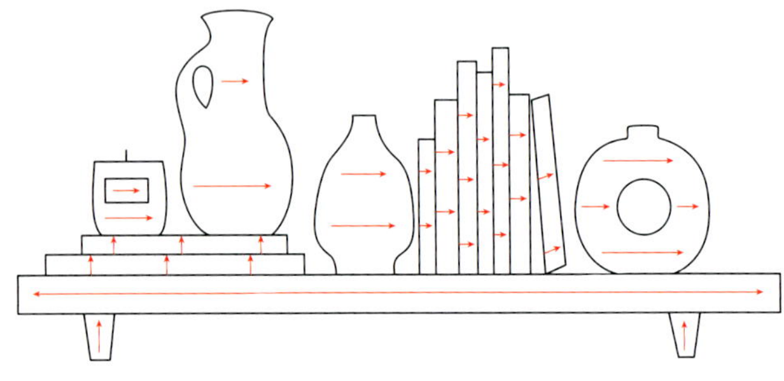

G

SHELF

1. Fill the shelf with rows of split backstitch in 435.

2. Fill each item on the shelf with satin stitches. Use tiny horizontal stitches for the books, and refer to the color guide for each thread color. Fill the candle with 543. Fill the candle label with BLANC. Fill the big jug with 739. Fill the middle vase with 3864 and the donut vase with BLANC. **H**

BACKGROUND

1. Stitch the floor with rows of horizontal split backstitch in 3864. **I**

2. Stitch the background wall with vertical rows of split backstitch in 712. Keep all the stitching vertical, even in the small spaces around the plants. **J**

I

J

TIP • It's useful to actually draw stitch direction guidelines onto the fabric, particularly for large spaces, before you start stitching so you can keep the stitching straight. Use the ruler and fineline pen.

Woven Elements

LAMPSHADES

Stitch the lampshades with a basic weave stitch on the diagonal and 3 strands of thread. Stitch one section of the lampshade at a time.

1. Stitch parallel diagonal straight stitches in 435, leaving roughly a 1mm gap between each stitch. **K**

2. Starting in the middle of the section, bring the needle up through the fabric, weave a length of 437 in a perpendicular diagonal row, and then bring the needle back down through the fabric. Use your needle to adjust the woven strand. The first woven strand is the most important, as it sets up the correct angle for the rest of the weave. **L**

3. Weave in the rest of the lampshade, filling the left side, then moving back to the center and weaving on the right side. **M** **N**

4. Repeat Step 3 to weave all the sections of the lampshade. Repeat on the second lampshade. **O**

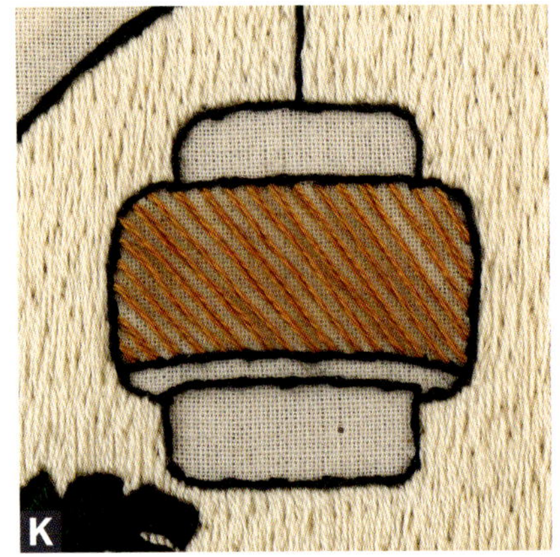

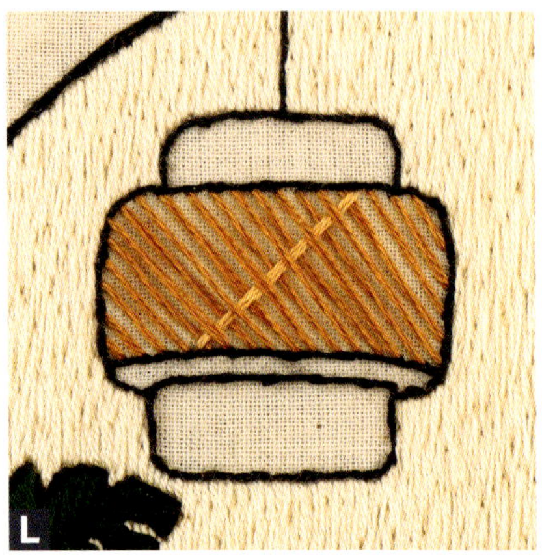

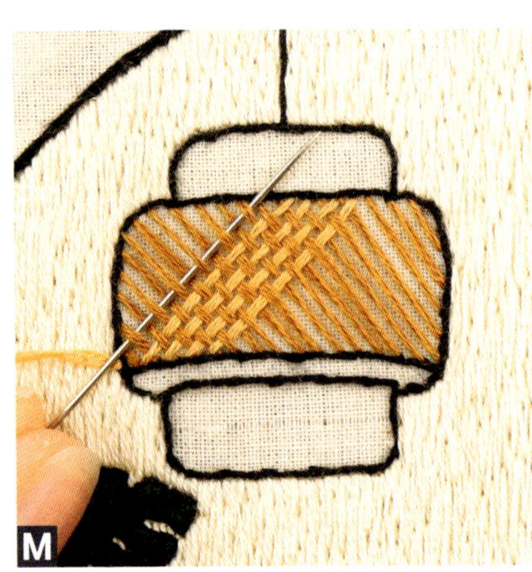

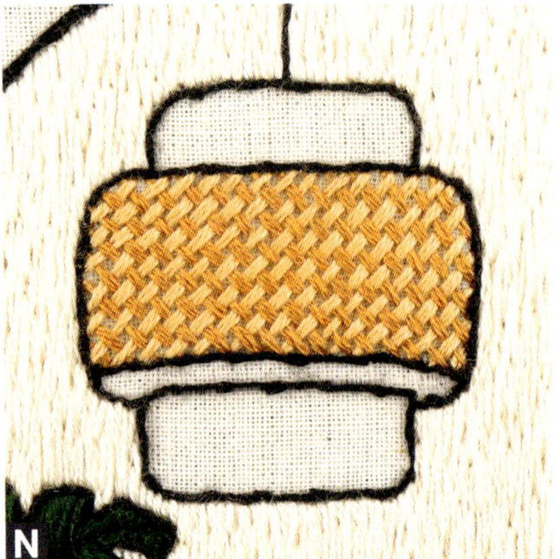

RUG

Create a wide-weave effect by using multiple straight stitches in each section. Use 3 strands of 437.

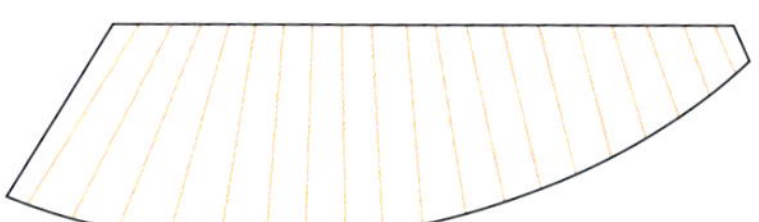

Rug vertical stitch direction

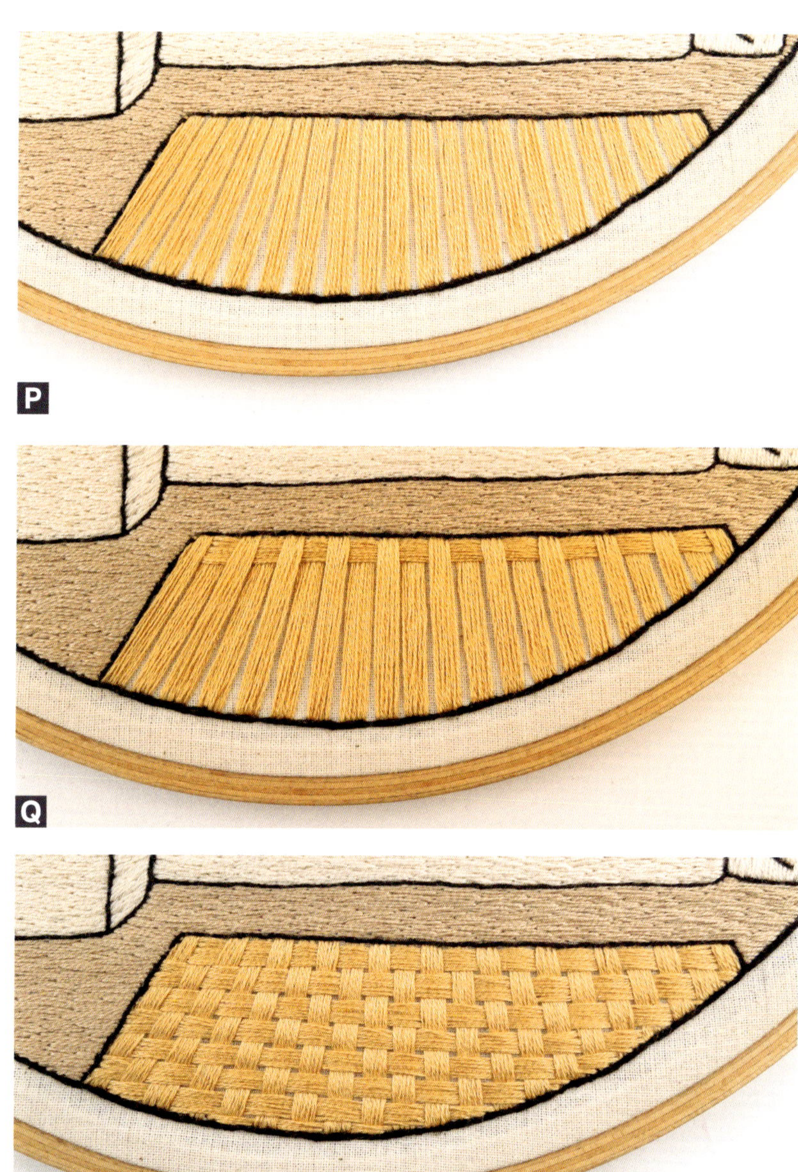

1. Stitch the vertical stitches. Stitch blocks of 5 straight stitches with a 1mm gap between each block of stitches. Slightly angle the blocks of stitches so they splay out around the curve, achieving perspective. Draw the stitch direction guide onto the rug shape to show you the angles if needed. **P**

2. Bring the needle up through the fabric and start weaving the horizontal lengths from the top right corner to the top left corner. Weave the same over/under pattern 5 times, creating a block of 5 lines. **Q**

3. Leave a 1mm gap, then repeat Step 2 with an opposite weave pattern for 5 lines. Continue until the rug is filled in. **R**

TIP • As you weave, turn the hoop to get easier angles!

CUSHIONS

Cushion 1

This pillow uses basic weave stitch with 2 colors.

1. Thread one needle with BLANC and another needle with 712. Stitch vertical straight stitches on the far left pillow: 2 in BLANC, 2 in 712 repeated across the cushion in line with the angle of the pillow shape. **A**

2. Weave the horizontal lengths. Weave 2 lengths of BLANC, then 2 lengths of 712 until the cushion is filled. **B**

A

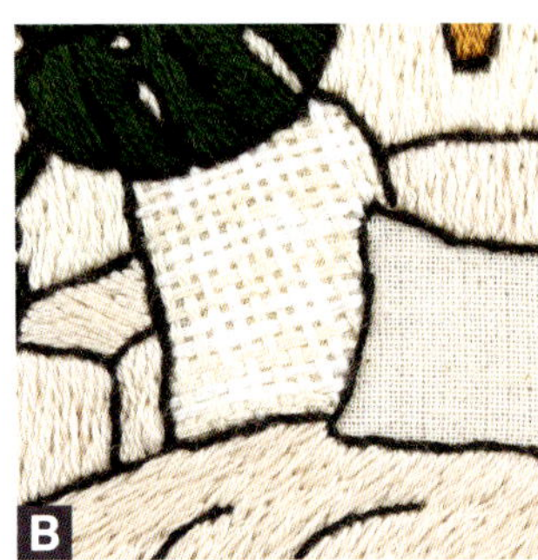

B

Cushion 2

This pillow uses ribbed weave stitch.

1. Stitch vertical straight stitches of 738 across the cushion shape, roughly 2mm apart and in line with the pillow shape. **C**

2. Bring the needle up through the fabric at the top right corner of the cushion. Weave the needle under the first vertical stitch. Bring the needle back in front of the first vertical stitch, then weave the needle under the first 2 vertical stitches. **D**

3. Bring the needle back in front of the second vertical stitch, then weave the needle under the second and third vertical stitches. Repeat to finish the row, looping around each stitch before going under 2 stitches. Stitch back down through the fabric at the end of the row. Don't pull too hard on the thread. **E**

4. Always work rows right to left. Repeat Steps 2–3 to fill the pillow with rows of ribbed weave stitch. **F**

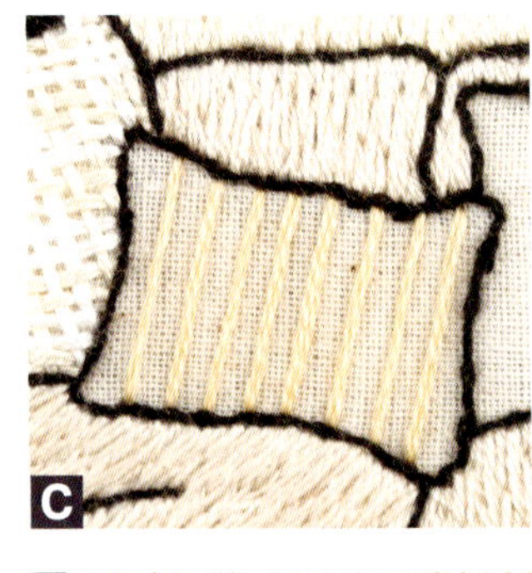

C

D

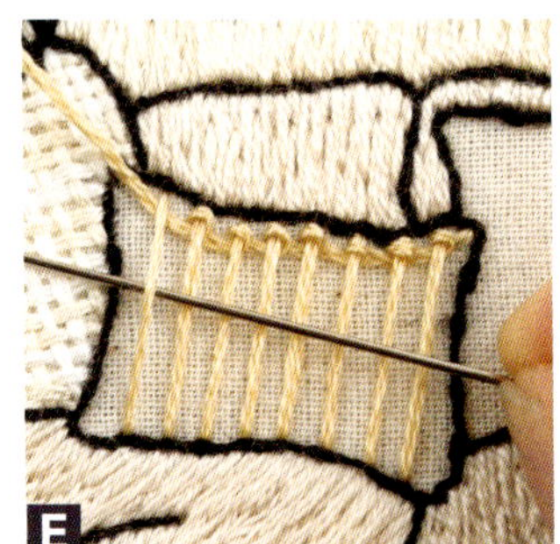

E

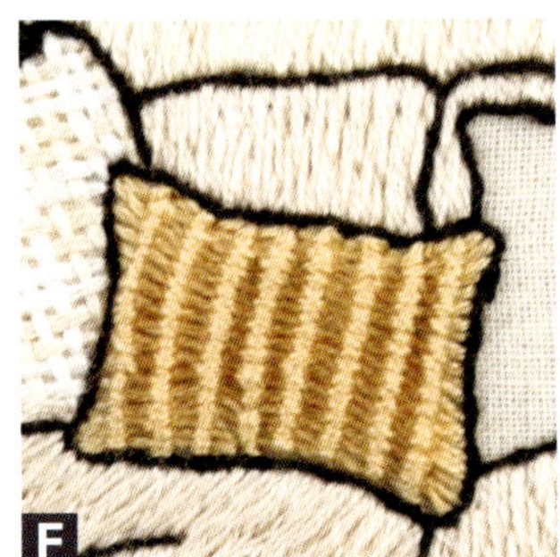

F

Cushion 3

If you feel a bit intimidated by ceylon stitch, swap it for rows of chain stitches to achieve a similar "knitted" texture!

1. Use 6 strands of 739. Backstitch two rows at the top and bottom of the shape. G

2. Make the first row of ceylon loops at the top. H

3. Continue to make rows of loops to fill the pillow. Use a pin or a finger to hold the loops flat. I

4. When there is space for only one more row of loops, stitch them through the bottom row of backstitches. J

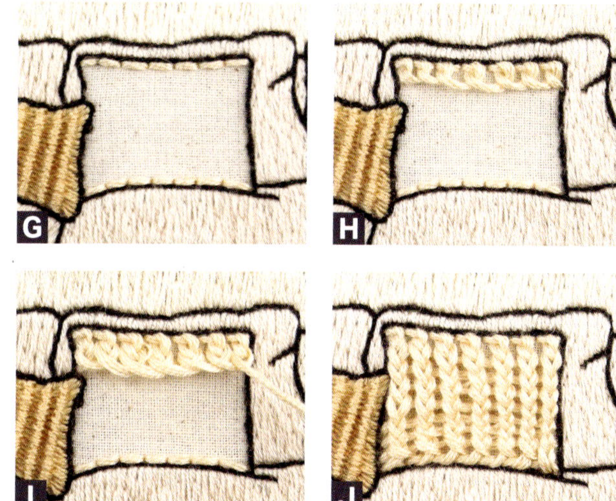

Cushion 4

This cushion is essentially a large woven wheel, with the corners woven to fill out the square shape.

1. Using 3 strands of 3864, stitch 8 radial straight stitches from the middle to the 4 corners and 4 sides. Stitch one more spoke somewhere on the pillow so there are 9. K

2. Coming up through the fabric from the center of the framework, weave under and over the strands, going around the shape. L

3. Weave the woven wheel until the diameter of the circle touches the edges of the cushion. Keep the tension loose and use a finger to flatten the thread into place. Bring the needle back down through the fabric. M

4. Stitch 2 more straight stitches in 1 corner, on either side of the existing framework stitch. N

5. Bring the needle up through the fabric where the wheel meets the edge of the cushion. Weave the thread over/under the 3 stitches until you fill the corner. O

6. Repeat Steps 4–5 in the other 3 corners. P

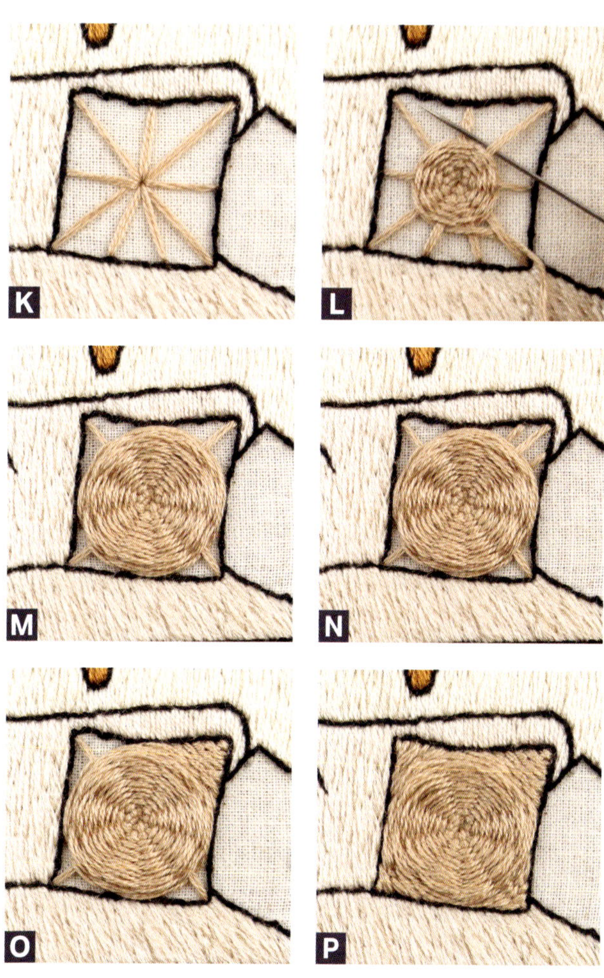

Cushion 5

Repeat all steps from Cushion 1 (page 50) to weave the final cushion. Q R

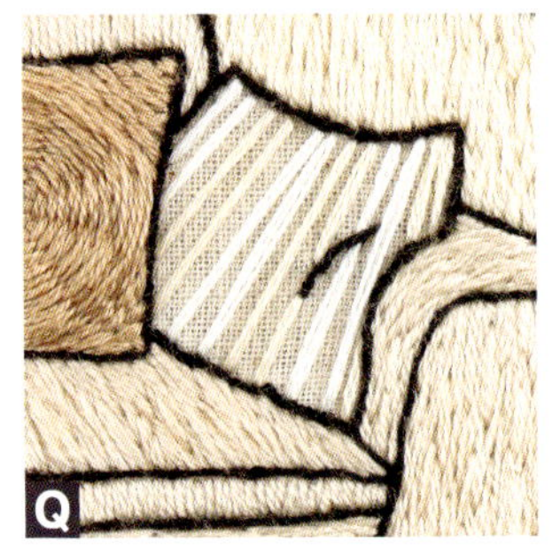
Q

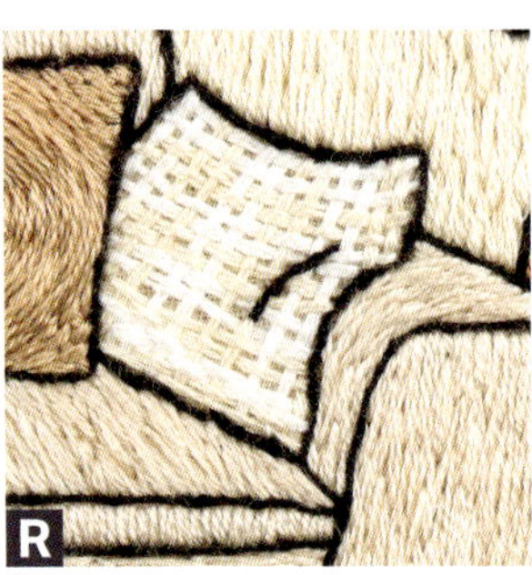
R

WOVEN WALL HANGING

Prepare

1. Create the mini cardboard loom. Draw ½" (1.2cm) guidelines at the top and bottom of the 2¾" × 4" (7cm × 10cm) rectangle of cardboard. Cut 12 notches in the middle of both the top and bottom of the piece of cardboard, ⅛" (3mm) apart and ½" deep (using the guidelines to show where to stop). Make sure the notches at the top and bottom align. A

A

2. String the loom using BLANC pearl cotton. Thread the cotton through the bottom left notch, leaving a tail of 2" at the back of the cardboard. Tape this tail to the back. Pull the cotton up into the top left notch, then string it from top to bottom, then bottom to top, creating small loops on the backs of the notches. Tape the other end to the back. B C

B

C

12 parallel lengths of cotton

Weave

1. Cut a length of the BLANC tapestry yarn and thread onto the tapestry needle. Starting at the top guideline, use the needle to go under and over the lengths of cotton from right to left. Pull the yarn through, leaving a tail of a few inches at the end. **D**

2. Repeat going back the other way, going over and under the opposite lengths of string. Don't pull too hard on the yarn; be very gentle to avoid warping the weaving. Adjust the line so it lays neatly. Repeat to weave 4 rows (approximately ⅜" or 1cm). Leave a tail on one side. **E**

3. Repeat Step 2 with Eco Vita yarn 002. Weave until the section measures ¾" (1.9cm). If you run out of yarn, leave a tail on one side and continue with a new length of yarn. **F**

4. Repeat Step 2 with 203. Weave until the section measures ⅜" (1cm). **G**

5. At the bottom, tie 4" (10cm) lengths of BLANC tapestry yarn around each warp string. **H**

6. Weave the loose yarn tails into the weaving by threading them on the needle and weaving them into the matching color section. Trim the rest of the tail. **I**

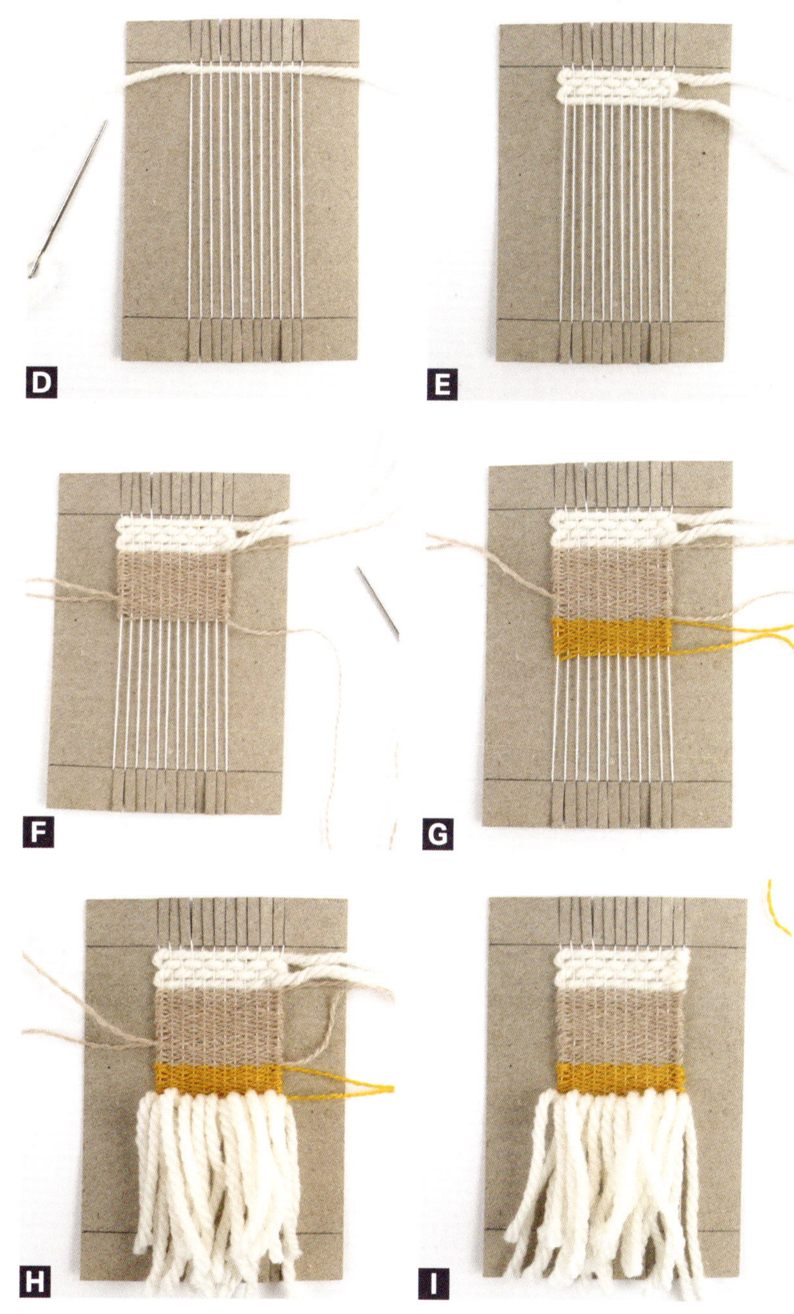

7. Remove the weaving from the loom, carefully releasing the loops. Add the dowel through the loops at the top. **J**

8. Cut the loops at the bottom, tie them together, then trim the excess away. **K**

9. Trim the BLANC yarn fringe at the bottom to ¾" (1.9cm) long. **L**

TIP • To keep the yarns in place and set the yarn fibers, lightly spray the wall hanging with hairspray.

10. Stitch the woven wall hanging onto the embroidery using 4 straight stitches of BLANC pearl thread, one at each corner. **M**

11. Finish the hoop using your preferred finishing method (see Display and Finishing, page 36).

J

K

L

M

Make It Your Own!

PICOT CRAZY

If you want even more woven elements in the design, why not try swapping out the monstera and cactus plants for huge picot leaves in varied shades of green (see Woven Trellis, page 31)!

CHANGE THE COLORS

Cool and calm colors not your thing? Stitch the design using bright shades instead! Oranges, yellows, and teals create a 70s vibe. Use multiple thread colors for the rug. Switch the woven wall hanging for a miniature picture frame (see Gallery Dining Room, Frames, page 90).

Finished size: 7″ hoop

Textured Bedroom

The bedroom is the coziest, most comfortable room in the house! It's the perfect place to snuggle up and rest. Textures are so important to making a space feel balanced and cozy. This project uses a variety of stitches in order to achieve a textured and interesting embroidery.

TOOLS & MATERIALS

$10\frac{1}{2}$″ × $10\frac{1}{2}$″ (26.7cm × 26.7cm) lightweight cotton linen fabric in a light neutral color

7″ (17.8cm) embroidery hoop

Embroidery needle (size 5)

Sewing pins

Dried flowers

Small scrap of paper

Textured Bedroom Template (page 40)

THREAD

1 ball DMC pearl cotton, 310 (size 12)

DMC 6-strand embroidery floss

- 3362 (dark green)—2 skeins
- 739 (pale yellow, or a color that matches the dried flowers)—1 skein
- 06 (pink-grey)—2 skeins
- 3826 (orange)—1 skein
- 680 (mustard yellow)—1 skein
- 3364 (dusty green)—1 skein
- BLANC (white)—1 skein
- 407 (dusty pink)—1 skein
- 300 (red-brown)—1 skein
- 823 (navy blue)—1 skein
- E317 (metallic silver)—1 skein
- 469 (green)—1 skein

STITCHES USED

Split Backstitch (page 23)

Satin Stitch (page 23)

Chain Stitch (page 24)

Turkeywork (page 27)

French Knots (page 25)

Woven Trellis Stitch (page 31)

Couching Stitch (page 28)

for Poetry
Crane

Outline

1. Load the fabric onto the hoop, and tighten the screw so the fabric tension is like the surface of a drum (see Prepare the Hoop, page 16).

2. Transfer the design onto the fabric (see Transfer Methods, page 18). I use the wash-away transfer paper method. **A**

3. Stitch all the outlines in split backstitch with 1 strand of 310 pearl thread. **B**

4. If you're using dissolvable transfer paper, remove the fabric from the hoop, and wash away the paper. Wait for the fabric to fully dry, iron it flat, then load the fabric back into the hoop. As you tighten, make sure that the straight lines of stitching are still straight.

5. Optional: If you plan to finish the project using the seal-in-the-hoop method (page 36), trim the outer skirt of fabric to 1″ (2.5cm). Then, using 1 strand of the 310 pearl thread, stitch around the outline circle with split backstitch, stitching through the fabric skirt. **C**

A

B

C

Color guide

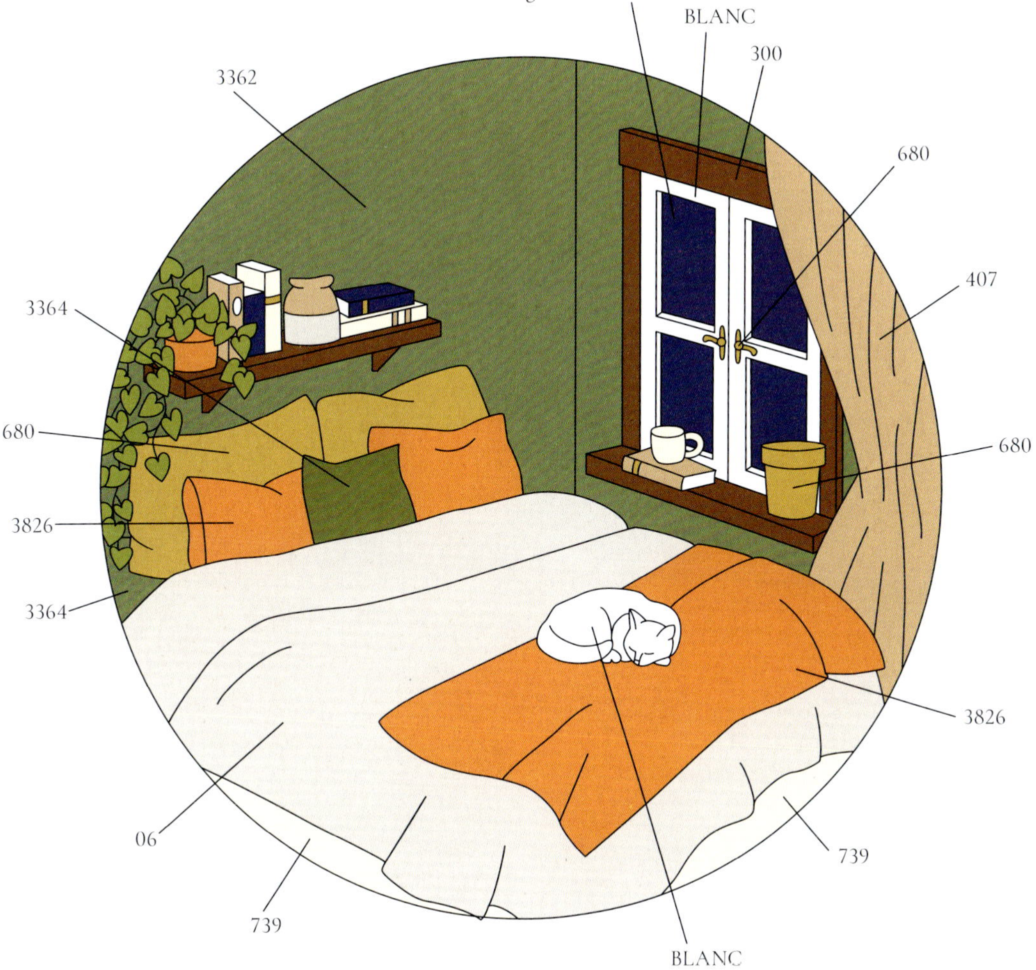

823
BLANC
300
3362
680
407
3364
680
680
3826
3364
3826
06
739
739
BLANC

Detail color guides

739
407
407
680
06
680
823
407
469
823
BLANC
739
300
3826

739
680
407
BLANC

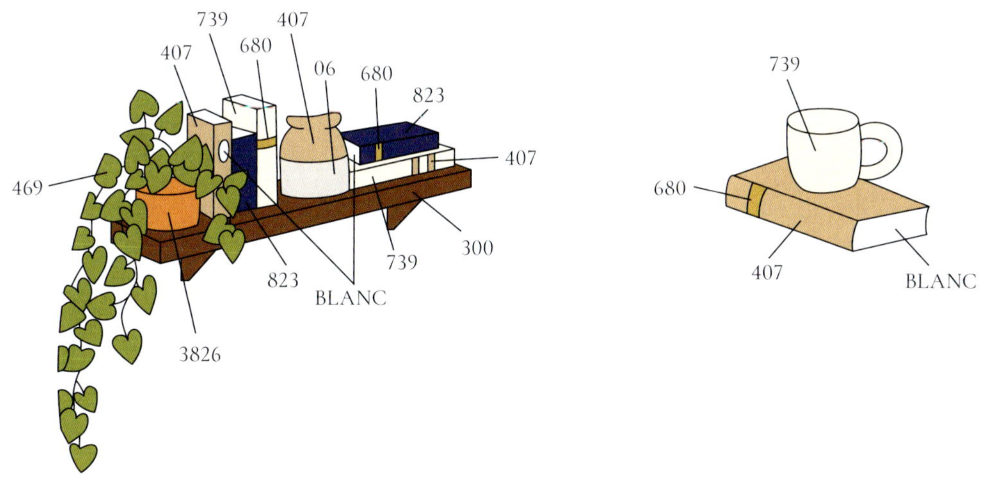

Fill Color

Unless otherwise stated, use 3 strands of embroidery floss to fill the color. Stay inside the stitched outlines. Refer to the color guides (page 59) and stitch direction guides in each section as needed. Make sure to follow the stitching order of the instructions. In particular, wait until the very end to add the delicate dried flowers.

BACKGROUND

1. Stitch the background with a split backstitch in 3362. Work in vertical rows, following the stitch direction guide. **A**

2. Stitch the floor with split backstitch in 739. **B**

A

B

TIP • Draw guidelines with a ruler and pen before stitching to help keep large blocks of stitching going in the right direction.

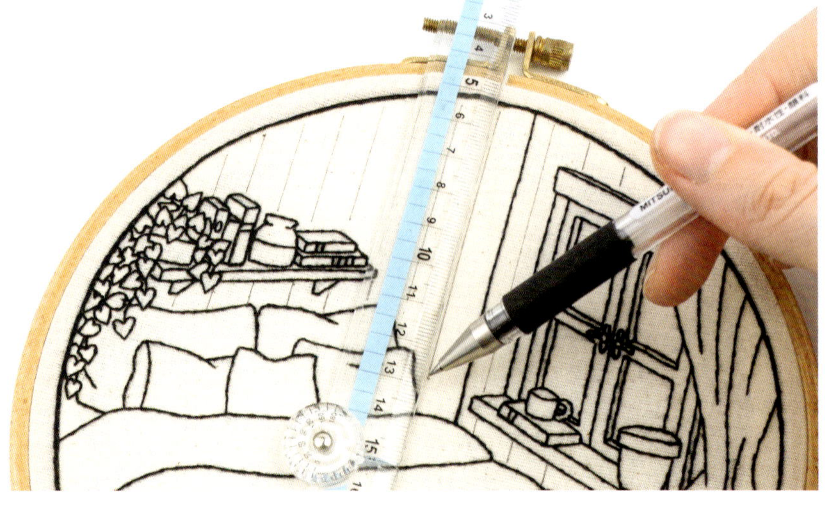

BED & CAT

1. Satin stitch the folded top of the duvet in 06. Split backstitch the rest of the duvet in the same color. Refer to the stitch direction guide to curve the stitching. **C**

2. Use 6 strands of 3826 to chain stitch the blanket. Work in rows from the top of the blanket to the bottom, working around the cat. Slant and angle the rows to follow the flow of the blanket shape. **D** **E**

C

D

E

TIP • For more complicated stitches (like chain stitch, turkeywork, and french knots), use your spare hand to catch the loops as you stitch. Since you need two hands, you might want to use a hoop stand, or balance the hoop on a table edge.

3. Stitch turkeywork tassels in one row on the left end of the blanket using 3 strands of 3826. The loops should be about ½" (1.2cm) long. Trim the loops. **F** **G**

4. Padded satin stitch the two small pillows in 3826. Stitch horizontal straight stitches across the pillows, then add vertical satin stitches on top. Stitch the thin left edge of the left pillow with horizontal satin stitch. **H**

5. Stitch the larger pillows in 680 with horizontal rows of french knots. **I**

6. Stitch rows of turkeywork in 3364 to fill the central square cushion. Leave 1/10" (3mm) space between the rows. Trim the loops a little shorter than the blanket tassels. Use a finger to fluff up the threads. **J** **K**

7. Stitch the small corner of the sheet with horizontal satin stitches in 3364. **L**

8. Stitch the cat with split backstitch in BLANC. Refer to the stitch direction guide and curve the split backstitch to the shape of the cat. **M**

WINDOW

1. Stitch the curtain using horizontal satin stitch in 407. **A**

2. Split backstitch the window frame and shelf in 300. Split backstitch the window panels in BLANC. Vertical satin stitch the sky outside the window in 823. **B**

3. Add silver stars to the sky using French knots with 2 strands of E317 metallic thread (suggested placement indicated by the green crosses on the stitch direction guide). **C**

TIP • Metallic thread can be frustrating to work with. Keep the lengths of thread short, and cut the strand if it gets tangled. Alternatively, you could use silver seed beads for stars.

4. Satin stitch the window accessories. Use 739 for the mug, 407 for the book cover, BLANC for the book pages, and 680 for the spine stripe. Stitch the plant pot and the window handles in 680. **D**

5. To stitch the mini palm on the windowsill, stitch 5 turkeywork loops in 3364, starting at the edge of the plant pot and going up to a pin at the edge of the curtain. Make sure the loops start and finish in roughly the same place. **E**

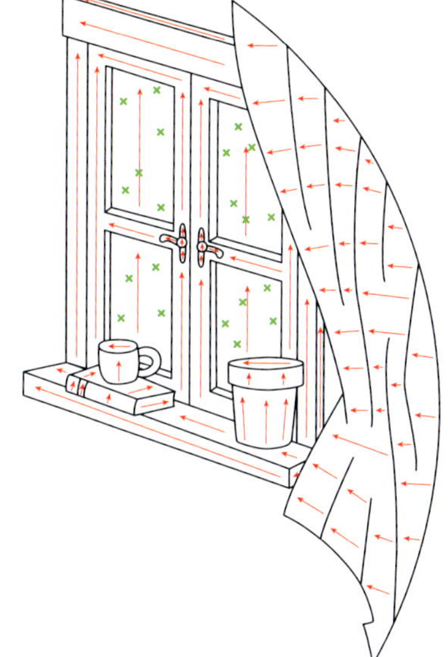

A

B

C

D

E

6. Starting from the edge of the plant pot, couch stitch over the tassels in 3826 to create stems. Stitch until halfway up the tassels. F

7. Repeat Steps 6–7 to add a second palm over the top of the curtain as shown. Cut both sets of loops, then fluff. G

F

G

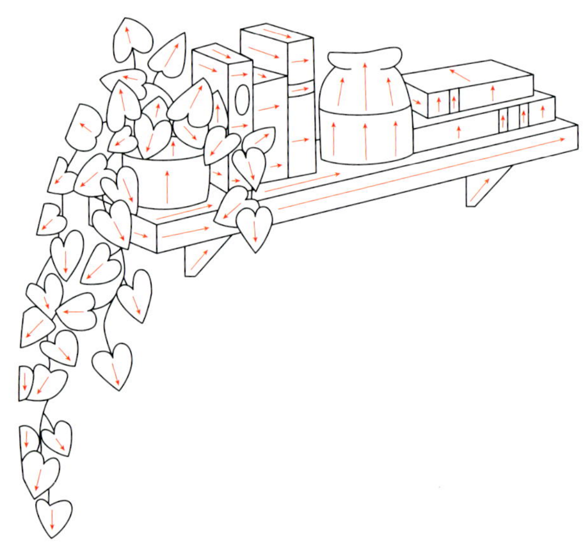

SHELF

1. Stitch the shelf with split backstitch in 300. A

2. Satin stitch the ivy leaves in 469. B

3. Satin stitch the books following the detail color guide. Satin stitch the plant pots. Use 3826 for the ivy pot and 407 and 06 for the mason jar. C

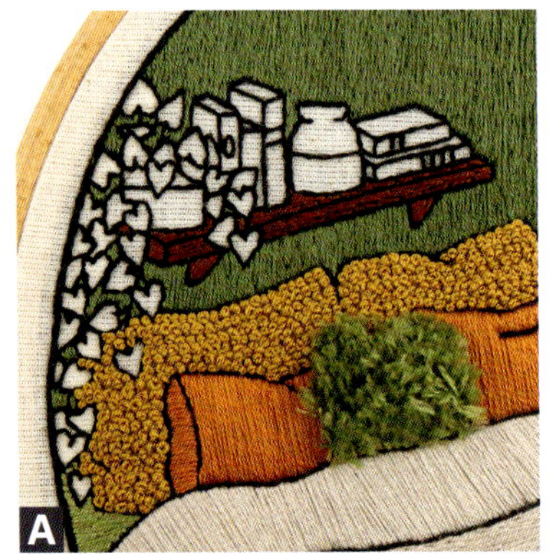

A

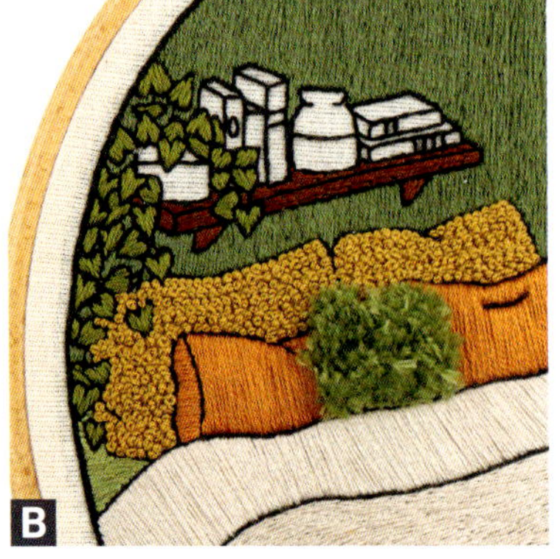

B

C

4. Pin a slip of scrap paper above the shelf. This makes it easier to weave the trellis leaves on top of the previously stitched background. Stitch a woven trellis triangle framework in 3364 emerging from the mason jar to the left. **D**

5. Weave the leaf from top to bottom, adjusting the thread with the needle as needed. Remove the pin. **E**

6. Repeat Steps 4–5 to add 2 more leaves behind the first. Fold the existing leaves down as you add new ones. The second leaf should lean to the right side, and the third should be centered. **F** **G**

D

E

F

G

DRIED FLOWERS

Any dried flowers can look interesting in this project. These dried reeds look like rush stems in proportion to this design!

1. Arrange the dried flowers on the hoop in the corner of the room.

2. Couch stitch over the stems using 2 strands of a matching color; I am using 739. **A**

3. Cut the ends of the stems so it appears as if they come from behind the bed. **B**

4. Finish the hoop using your preferred finishing method (see Display and Finishing, page 36).

A

B

Make It Your Own!

PATTERNED BACKGROUND

Stitch on floral fabric to create a more heavily patterned background. Don't stitch the background over the fabric. Match the thread colors to the colors in the fabric. Add 3D elements to create more dimension.

CHUNKIER YARN

Stitch all of the color with tapestry thread or 6 strands of embroidery thread for a chunkier feel. Enlarge the pattern and stitch only a 4" x 6" (10.2 × 15.2cm) section to fit into a frame.

Finished size: 8″ hoop

Family Kitchen

The most important part of the home is the people who inhabit it. Stitching people can feel intimidating, but this project will show you tips and tricks for embroidering humans. There are so many beautiful details which add up to an intricate scene of everyday life. The key to stitching small details, such as faces or leaves, is to keep your stitches small and tight. Stitching a curved line simply means using lots of tiny straight stitches. It takes time and patience, but the results are amazing.

TOOLS & MATERIALS

11½″ × 11½″ (29cm × 29cm) lightweight cotton linen fabric in a light neutral color

8″ (20cm) wooden embroidery hoop

Embroidery needle (size 5)

Family Kitchen Template (page 40)

THREAD

1 ball DMC pearl cotton, 310 (size 12)

DMC 6-strand embroidery floss

- 3770 (pale pink)—1 skein
- 801 (dark brown)—1 skein
- 434 (mid brown)—1 skein
- BLANC (white)—1 skein
- 436 (mid pale brown)—1 skein
- 3371 (very dark brown)—1 skein
- 938 (mid dark brown)—1 skein
- 3760 (bright blue)—1 skein
- 3753 (pale blue)—2 skeins
- 844 (dark grey)—1 skein
- 3853 (bright orange)—1 skein
- 321 (red)—1 skein
- 3825 (peach)—1 skein
- 950 (pale peach)—2 skeins
- 3750 (navy blue)—1 skein
- 728 (bright yellow)—1 skein
- 745 (pale yellow)—1 skein
- 169 (pale blue-grey)—1 skein
- 3345 (dark green)—1 skein
- 740 (dusty orange)—1 skein
- 988 (bright green)—1 skein
- 3013 (pale green)—1 skein

STITCHES USED

Split Backstitch (page 23)

Satin Stitch (page 23)

French Knots (page 25)

Outline

1. Load the fabric onto the hoop, and tighten the screw so the fabric tension is like the surface of a drum (see Prepare the Hoop, page 16).

2. Transfer the design onto the fabric (see Transfer Methods, page 18). I use the wash-away transfer paper method. **A**

3. Stitch all the outlines in split backstitch with 1 strand of 310 pearl thread. Use very small stitches to achieve the small details. Work on 1 element at a time. **B**

4. If you're using dissolvable transfer paper, remove the fabric from the hoop, and wash away the paper. Wait for the fabric to fully dry, iron it flat, then load the fabric back into the hoop. As you tighten, make sure that the straight lines of stitching are still straight.

5. Optional: If you plan to finish the project using the seal-in-the-hoop method (page 36), trim the outer skirt of fabric to 1˝ (2.5cm). Then, using 1 strand of the 310 pearl thread, stitch around the outline circle with split backstitch, stitching through the fabric skirt. **C**

A

B

C

Color guide

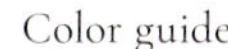

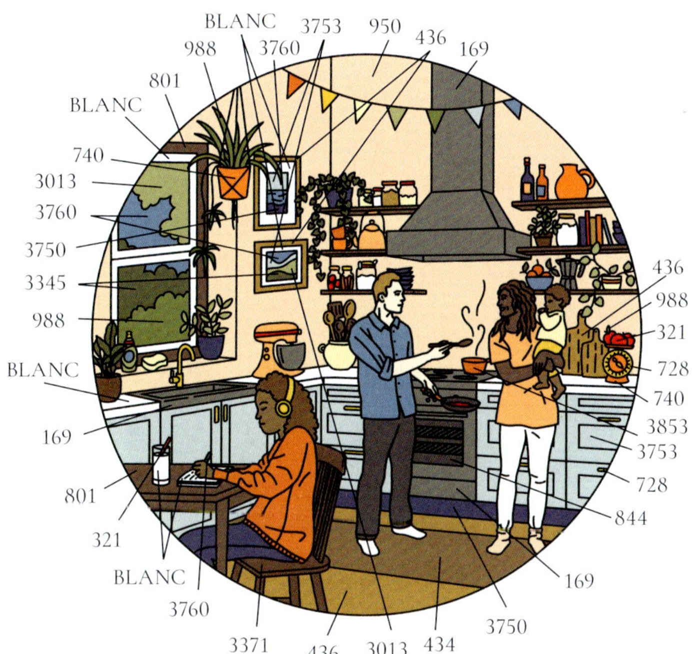

Detail color guides

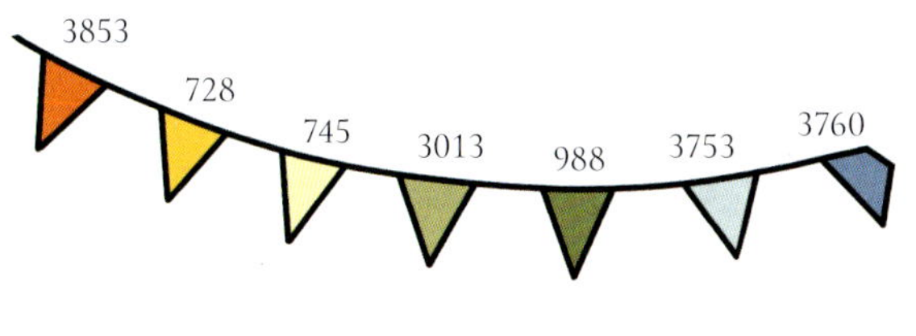

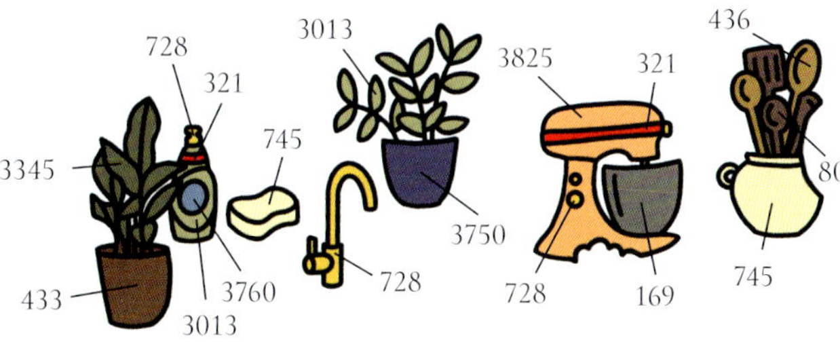

Fill Color

Unless otherwise stated, use 3 strands of embroidery floss to fill the color. Stay inside the stitched outlines. Refer to the color guides (page 71) and stitch direction guides in each section as needed.

All of the colors in this design are used in multiple places. These instructions will guide step by step through each area, but if you don't want to keep cutting the thread and changing colors so often, you can stitch all the areas that use the same color at once, like an embroidered color-by-number!

FAMILY

1. Stitch the skin of each person. Use 3770 for the man, 801 for the woman, and 434 for the children. Use only 2 strands of thread for the faces and fingers. Stitch the faces with small, vertical rows of satin stitches. Split backstitch the arms and the baby's legs. Stitch 1 tiny straight stitch using 1 strand of BLANC for the woman's mouth. If the black outlines get lost, use the needle to pull the outline thread up. Single stitches should be enough to fill thin spaces. **A B**

A

B

2. Satin stitch the man's hair with 436. Split backstitch the woman's hair with 3371 to create waves. Stitch French knots for the hair of both children with 938 to create curly hair. C

3. Split backstitch the man's clothes, following the stitch direction guide and shape of the clothing. Use 3760 for the shirt, 844 for the pants, and BLANC for the socks. Satin stitch the pan he's holding with 844, 3853, and 321. Satin stitch the wooden spoon with 801. D

4. Split backstitch the women's clothes. Use 3825 for her T-shirt, BLANC for her pants, and 950 for her socks. E

5. Split backstitch the girl's clothes. Use 3853 for her sweater, 3750 for her pants, and 728 for her headphones. F

6. Split backstitch the baby's clothes. Use 745 for his top and 728 for his pants. G

BACKGROUND

1. Stitch the cupboard doors with 3753. Use split backstitch in rows on the panel frames as indicated by the stitch direction guide. Satin stitch the center of the panels. Satin stitch the handles in 728. Split backstitch the countertops in BLANC. Split backstitch the baseboards in 3750. **A**

2. Split backstitch the sink, oven, and hood in 169. **B**

3. Continue to fill the following objects in satin stitch using the color guides: saucepan, apples, plant leaves.

4. Continue to fill the following objects in split backstitch using the color guides: stove burners, oven interior, plant pot, sink faucet, mixer, spoon jar and spoons, cutting boards, scale. **C**

A

B

C

Shelves

1. Split backstitch the shelves in 801. **D**

2. Leave the upper areas of each glass jar empty. Fill the teapot and contents of each jar on the shelves using split backstitch, referring to the color and stitch direction guides.

3. Fill the remaining objects on the shelves using satin stitch and referring to the color and stitch direction guides. **E**

D

E

Remaining Details

1. Split backstitch the table in 801, the chair in 3371, the girl's book and glass of milk in BLANC, the pen in 3760, and the straw in 321. **F**

F

2. Split backstitch the outer window frame in 801 and the inner frame in BLANC. Satin stitch the sky in 3760. G

3. Split backstitch the trees in 988, 3345, and 3013. Achieve the 'leafy' texture by following the curved outlines of the trees with curved rows of split backstitch, until the rows completely fill the shape. G

4. Satin stitch the windowsill plant and sponge. Split backstitch the liquid soap. Follow the color and stitch direction guides. G

5. Satin stitch the hanging spider plant pot in 740. Split backstitch the plant in 988. Split backstitch the frames following the stitch and color guides. Satin stitch the paintings following the stitch and color guides. H

6. Satin stitch colorful bunting in the following colors: 3853, 728, 745, 3013, 988, 3753, 3760. I

7. Split backstitch the floor in 436 and 434. J

8. Stitch the walls with vertical rows of split backstitch in 950. Fill in all the tiny gaps around the objects, including the interior of the jars. K

9. Finish the hoop using your preferred finishing method (see Display and Finishing, page 36).

Make It Your Own!

CUSTOMIZE THE PEOPLE

Turn a photograph of a person into an embroidery outline by tracing it!

1. Select a photograph. Resize the image to fit into the embroidery template (digitally or manually). **A**

TIP • Does the design have a chair you want the person to sit in? Pose a willing model in a chair at the same angle, and take a photo!

2. Use tracing paper or a digital program like Photoshop or Procreate to trace an outline of the person. Try to keep the outline as simple as possible while still including key details. **B**

3. Print or trace the outline at the right size. Replace the existing person with the custom one. **C**

4. Stitch the new person first. Then, adjust the background pattern around it, adding or removing lines as needed so the new person blends in seamlessly. **D**

5. Continue to stitch the rest of the pattern, then dissolve any transfer paper, and stitch the color.

A

B

C

D

Smaller section of the embroidery is stitched to fit into this frame

Finished size: 7″ hoop

Beaded Bathroom

Everyone loves a bubble bath! Beautiful bathrooms are a true oasis away from the manic rush of everyday life. As such, this embroidered bathroom has been designed to exude peacefulness and luxury. Beading takes center stage, transforming this embroidered bathroom into a true showstopper by adding dimension, playfulness, and an undeniable sense of glam!

TOOLS & MATERIALS

10½″ × 10½″ (26.7cm × 26.7cm) lightweight cotton linen fabric in a light neutral color

7″ (17.8cm) wooden embroidery hoop

Embroidery needle (size 5)

Beading needle (size 12)

Ruler

Fineline pen

Beaded Bathroom Template (page 40)

THREAD

1 ball DMC pearl cotton, 310 (size 12)

DMC 6-strand embroidery floss

- 169 (blue-grey)—2 skeins
- 869 (dark brown)—1 skein
- 522 (dusty green)—1 skein
- 783 (mustard yellow)—1 skein
- BLANC (white)—3 skeins
- 168 (pale blue)—1 skein
- 471 (bottle green)—2 skeins
- 645 (grey)—1 skein
- 06 (pale pink-grey)—1 skein
- 167 (mid brown)—1 skein
- 895 (dark green)—1 skein
- 3826 (red-brown)—1 skein
- 369 (pale turquoise)—4 skeins
- 937 (mid-dark green)—1 skein

BEADS

40–50 white pearl-effect beads (5mm)

50–60 clear round beads (4mm)

200 white seed beads (2mm)

250 yellow seed beads (1.5mm)

100 turquoise seed beads (1.5mm)

15 bronze sequins (4mm)

25 bronze seed beads (1.5mm)

60 pale blue seed beads (2mm)

25 turquoise round beads (2mm)

60 green seed beads (1.5mm)

STITCHES USED

Split Backstitch (page 23)

Satin Stitch (page 23)

Basic Weave Stitch (page 28)

Beading (page 33)

Outline

1. Load the fabric onto the hoop, and tighten the screw so the fabric tension is like the surface of a drum (see Prepare the Hoop, page 16).

2. Transfer the design onto the fabric (see Transfer Methods, page 18). I use the wash-away transfer paper method. **A**

3. Stitch all the outlines in split backstitch with 1 strand of 310 pearl thread. **B**

4. If you're using dissolvable transfer paper, remove the fabric from the hoop, and wash away the paper. Wait for the fabric to fully dry, iron it flat, then load the fabric back into the hoop. As you tighten, make sure that the straight lines of stitching are still straight.

5. Optional: If you plan to finish the project using the seal-in-the-hoop method (page 36), trim the outer skirt of fabric to 1˝ (2.5cm). Then, using 1 strand of the 310 pearl thread, stitch around the outline circle with split backstitch, stitching through the fabric skirt. **C**

A

B

C

Color guide

Tile color guide

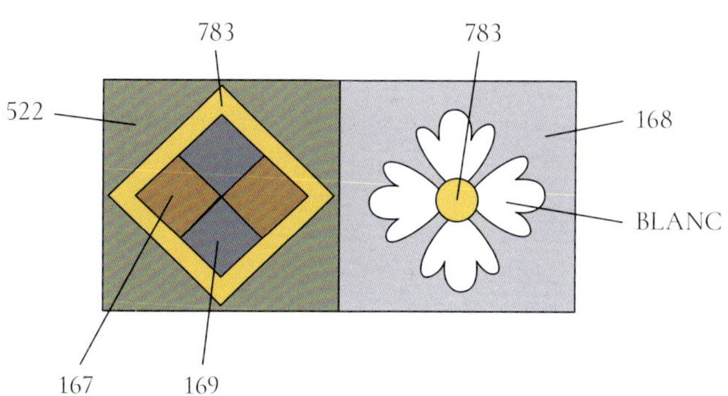

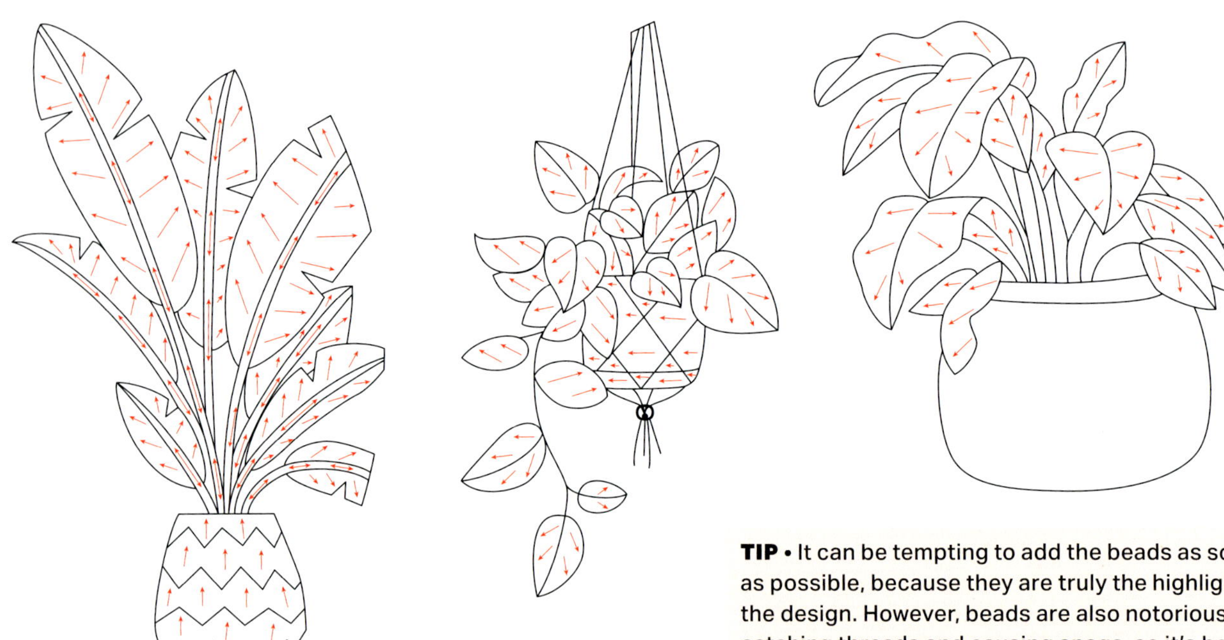

TIP • It can be tempting to add the beads as soon as possible, because they are truly the highlight of the design. However, beads are also notorious for catching threads and causing snags, so it's best to leave adding them until the end.

Fill Color

Unless otherwise stated, use 3 strands of embroidery floss to fill the color. Stay inside the stitched outlines. Refer to the color guides (page 81) and stitch direction guides in each section as needed.

PLANTS

1. Stitch the banana leaf plant, referring to the stitch direction guide. Start by filling the stems with split backstitch in 471. Then, use the same color to satin stitch the leaves, working from the stem to the outer edge. Fill the zigzag pot with vertical satin stitches in 783 and 168. **A** **B**

2. Satin stitch the hanging plant in 937. Stitch each leaf/half leaf outward from the center. Split backstitch horizontal rows in 783 and BLANC to stitch the hanging plant pot. **C**

3. Satin stitch the floor plant in 895, stitching outward from the center of each leaf. **D**

4. Weave stitch the basket of the floor plant using 6-strands of thread. Stitch vertical lines of 869, then weave horizontal rows of 167 starting at the top and working down. Add short vertical satin stitches to the rim in 869. **E**

BATHTUB

1. Satin stitch the inside, body, and rim of the bathtub with BLANC, referring to the stitch direction guide. Keep in mind that the beaded bubbles will cover much of the tub interior, but this bottom layer of stitches prevents any fabric from peeking through. **A**

2. Split stitch the bathtub details with 645 and BLANC, taking notice of the direction of the shapes to inform the direction and length of the stitches. Stitch the faucet pieces with a few horizontal stitches. **B**

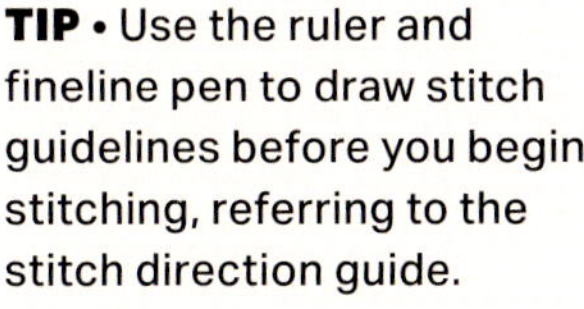

TIP • Use the ruler and fineline pen to draw stitch guidelines before you begin stitching, referring to the stitch direction guide.

BACKGROUND

1. Split backstitch the baseboard and upper shelf in 3826. A

2. Satin stitch the floor tiles in 06 and 169, referring to the stitch direction guide to match the slant of the tile shapes. B

3. Satin stitch the mint green wall tiles in 369. Work on one brick at a time. Stitch vertically, even when filling the more fiddly spaces around plant leaves. C

TIP • After you fill a lot of space with satin stitch, sometimes the original black outlines can get stitched over or lose some of their definition. Once the satin stitch is finished, if necessary, re-stitch over the outlines with the 310 pearl thread.

4. Stitch the patterned tiles, one color at a time, using satin stitch for all sections. Refer to the color and stitch direction guides. D E F

Beads

Now the fun begins! Change to a thinner beading needle. Use 1 strand of embroidery thread that matches the background thread color you're stitching into.

TILES

1. Using 1 strand of 783, stitch rows of yellow seed beads onto each straight edge of the diamonds. Bring the needle up at a corner, add the beads, measure how many are needed to fill the length, then secure at the other corner. Add anchoring stitches between each bead. Repeat for each row. A B

TIP • When you work on tiles which interact with the outer edge, or with the plants, decide if a bead will fit in the space or not. Omit them from any space that's too crowded!

2. Match up a bronze seed bead with a bronze sequin. Stitch them onto the 167 areas in the diamond tile, using 1 strand of 167. **C**

3. Add individual pale blue seed beads to the blue spaces inside the diamond. Stitch with 1 strand of 169.

4. At each corner of the diamond tiles, bead a row of 3 turquoise seed beads next to the row of yellow beads using 522. Add 1 more turquoise bead in the corner. **D**

TIP • Stitch 1 color of bead at a time, adding it across all the places it is used. Then, move onto the next bead.

5. Add 1 yellow seed bead in the center of each flower using 783 thread. **E**

6. On the petals, stitch rows of 2 white seed beads, and anchor them with BLANC thread. Add a turquoise round bead at each corner of the flower tiles with 168. Stitch green seed beads on either side of the turquoise beads using the same thread color. **F**

C

D

E

F

BUBBLES

Stitch with 1 strand of BLANC thread.

1. Start with the 5mm pearl-effect beads. Stitch them randomly over the inside of the bathtub and some in the space above it. **A**

2. Next, add the medium clear beads, filling in gaps. Stitch some below and around the rim of the bathtub, to create the illusion that the bubbles are overflowing and floating away! **B**

3. Fill in all remaining space with the tiny white seed beads. Add more floating above and below the main tub. *More is more* is the mantra here! **C**

4. Add more of all 3 types of beads on top of one another to make the effect even more three-dimensional. Don't try to make the beads flush with the fabric. Instead, as the thread is gently pulled back through the fabric, let the beads sit on top of other beads. **D**

ZIGZAG POT

1. Stitch single pale blue beads to the blue areas using 168 thread. A

2. Stitch bronze sequins and yellow seed beads onto the yellow areas with 783 thread. B

3. Finish the hoop using your preferred finishing method (see Display and Finishing, page 36).

A

B

Make It Your Own!

CHANGE THE COLORS

Your design will be unique to you depending on the beads and colors you choose. Stitch a different color scheme to get a completely different atmosphere and effect. Here, pearly pink beads are also used in the bubble bath, to reflect the pink tiles.

PAMPERED BATHER

Stitch a pampered lady into the bathtub with just her head and shoulders visible above the bubbles (see Customize the People, page 77). Consider cropping the design and displaying it in a funky frame!

Finished size: 8˝ hoop

Gallery Dining Room

A gallery wall is a celebration of artistic expression. In this embroidered dining room, it is a fabulous way to combine mixed media processes of painting and stitching. Adding some miniature frames also creates more fun and playfulness to this bright, cheerful dining room scene. The table is set for an inviting, colorful dinner party!

TOOLS & MATERIALS

11½˝ × 11½˝ (29cm × 29cm) lightweight cotton linen fabric in a light neutral color

8˝ (20.3cm) unvarnished wooden embroidery hoop

Dark brown acrylic paint

Flat paintbrush (size 8)

Embroidery needle (size 5)

Watercolor paints in various colors

Selection of small round paintbrushes

2 miniature frames 1¾˝ × 1¼˝ (4.3cm × 3.2cm)

Scrap paper

Ruler

Fineline pen

Craft glue (optional)

Gallery Dining Room Template (page 40)

THREAD

1 ball DMC pearl cotton, 310 (size 12)

DMC 6-strand embroidery floss

- BLANC (white)—1 skein
- 437 (pale brown)—1 skein
- 435 (mid brown)—1 skein
- 938 (dark brown)—1 skein
- 745 (pale yellow)—1 skein
- 3832 (hot pink)—1 skein
- 819 (pale pink)—3 skeins
- 3721 (burgandy-mauve)—2 skeins
- 469 (bottle green)—1 skein
- 372 (pale green)—1 skein
- 813 (blue)—1 skein
- 3753 (pale blue)—1 skein
- 991 (teal)—1 skein
- 782 (yellow) 1 skein

STITCHES USED

Split Backstitch (page 23)

Satin Stitch (page 23)

Detached Chain Stitch (page 25)

French Knots (page 25)

Padded Satin Stitch (page 24)

MINIATURE FRAMES

Miniature frames are available to buy online or from dollhouse supply stores. There are many varieties, from wooden and simple, to metallic and ornate.

Outline

1. Paint the outer ring of the embroidery hoop with the acrylic paint. Hold the hoop steady in one hand and paint around the screw, then paint the rest of the hoop. Wait for the paint to dry, then change where the hoop is held and finish painting the remaining area. Paint 2 coats, and let dry completely. **A**

2. Load the fabric onto the hoop, and tighten the screw so the fabric tension is like the surface of a drum (see Prepare the Hoop, page 16).

3. Transfer the design onto the fabric (see Transfer Methods, page 18). I use the wash-away transfer paper method. **B**

4. Stitch all the outlines in split backstitch with 1 strand of 310 pearl thread. **C**

5. If you're using dissolvable transfer paper, remove the fabric from the hoop, and wash away the paper. Wait for the fabric to fully dry, iron it flat, then load the fabric back into the hoop. As you tighten, make sure that the straight lines of stitching are still straight.

6. Optional: If you plan to finish the project using the seal-in-the-hoop method (page 36), trim the outer skirt of fabric to 1″ (2.5cm). Then, using 1 strand of the 310 pearl thread, stitch around the outline circle with split backstitch, stitching through the fabric skirt. **D**

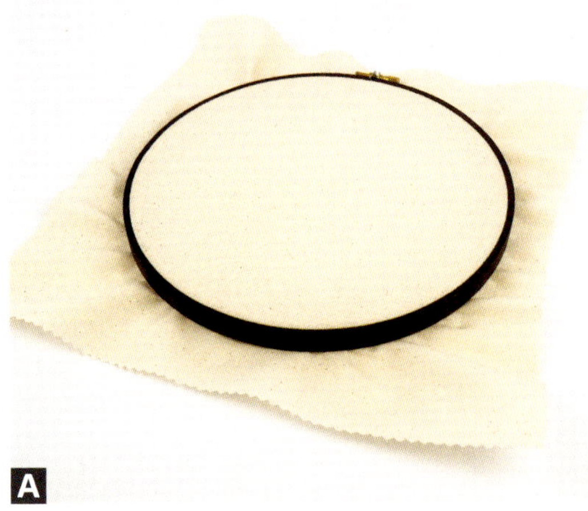
A

B

C

D

Color guide

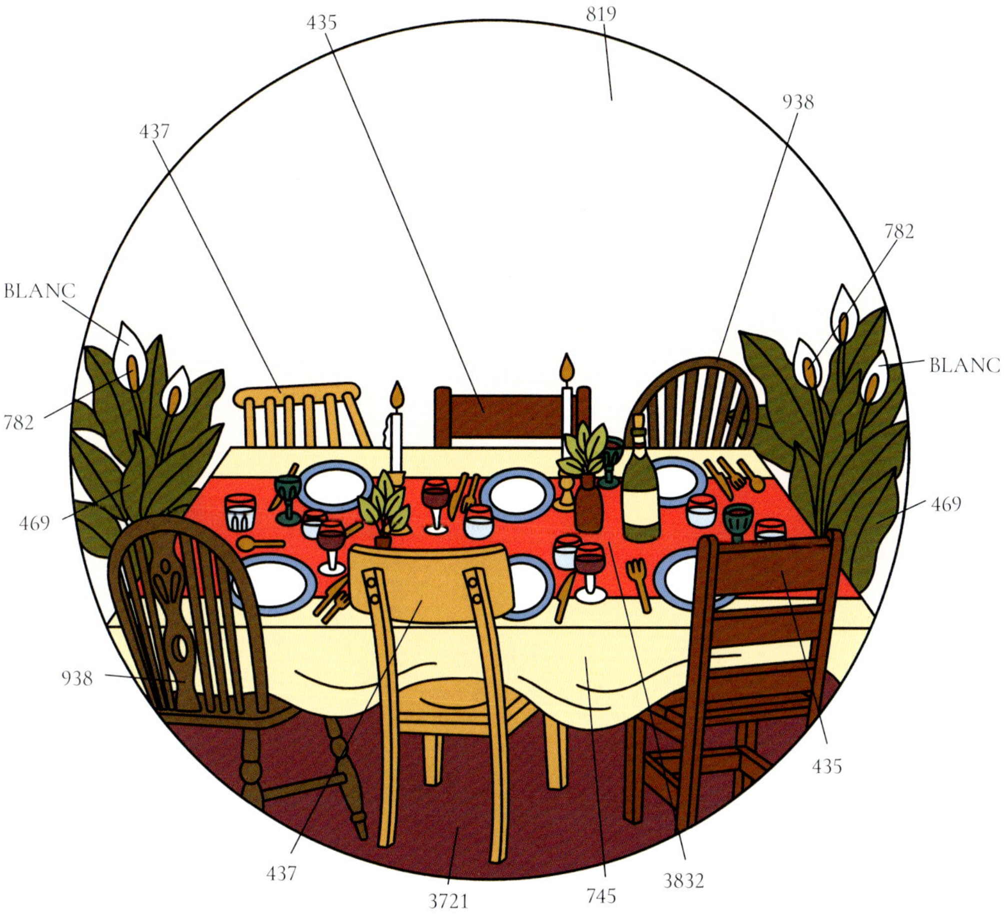
435
819
938
437
782
BLANC
BLANC
782
469
469
938
435
437
3721
745
3832

Detail color guide

782
BLANC
437
3721
372
469
745
782
991
3753
435
437
372
3721
BLANC
3753
991
782
813
3721

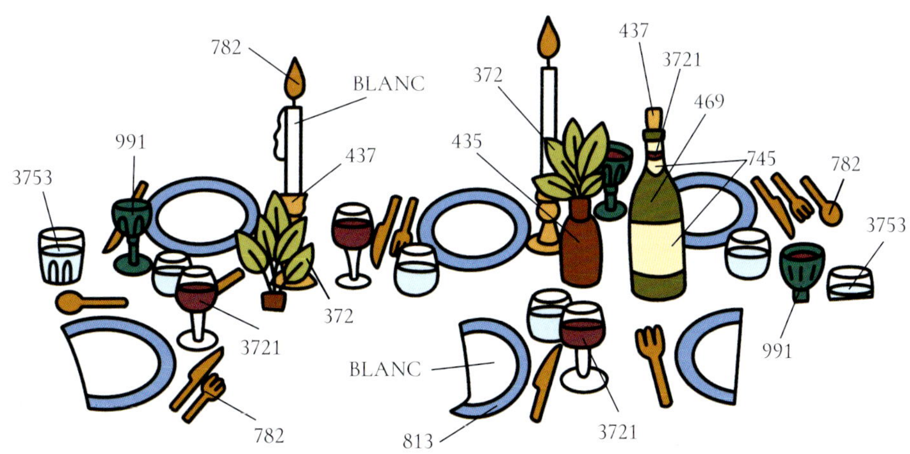

Art

Practice painting on a scrap of matching fabric before committing to painting on the actual embroidery.

1. Cut out rectangles of paper to fit on the walls with the miniature frames. Arrange the frames and paper shapes on the hoop to your liking, then trace around the frames and paper with the fineline pen. **A**

2. Use a ruler and the pen to draw inner frames and borders in all the rectangles. **B**

3. Paint the fabric to create the watercolor art. First, wet the fabric where you want to paint with a clean paintbrush. Then, layer and swirl the watercolors onto the wet area to create an abstract design. If the colors fade too much as they dry, add more paint.

Have fun playing with the watercolor paints, and the way the colors blend into each other. If a cohesive gallery wall is desired, use the same color palette in all the paintings. If a more eclectic vibe is preferred, go for different shades in each frame. It's ok for the paint to spill a little over the edges of the lines because they will be stitched over. Let dry completely. **C** **D**

Fill Color

Unless otherwise stated, use 3 strands of embroidery floss to fill the color. Stay inside the stitched outlines. Refer to the color guides (page 93) and stitch direction guides in each section as needed.

TABLE

Start by stitching the small details on the table.

1. Split backstitch the plates with BLANC thread, working in concentric circles from the outside to inside. Split backstitch the plate rims with 813. Add 5 detached chain stitches to create a flower in the center of each plate. If the plate is partially hidden add fewer petals. **A B**

2. Satin stitch the cutlery in 782. Each item will only need two or three stitches. **C**

3. Satin stitch the wine glass stems in BLANC. Follow the color guide to satin stitch the rest of the wine glasses with 991 (teal glass), 3753 (water), and 3721 (wine). Leave the tops of the glasses empty. **D**

4. Satin stitch the leaves on the table with 372 and the vases below with 435. Stitch the wine bottle with vertical satin stitches, following the color guide. Satin stitch the candle holders in 437, the candles in BLANC, and the flames in 782. **E**

5. Split backstitch horizontal rows for the tablecloth in 745. Repeat with 3832 for the table runner. Some areas will require very tiny stitches to fill small spaces in the correct direction. Follow the stitch direction guide for the shape of the fabric. **F** **G**

E

F

G

CHAIRS

1. Stitch the chairs in 938, 435 and 437 as shown in the color guide. Split backstitch the chairs in horizontal or vertical rows of stitching, referring to the stitch direction guide, to enhance the chair dimensions. **H**

TIP • If the black outline gets lost as you stitch the color, restitch over it with the 310 pearl thread to redefine the lines.

H

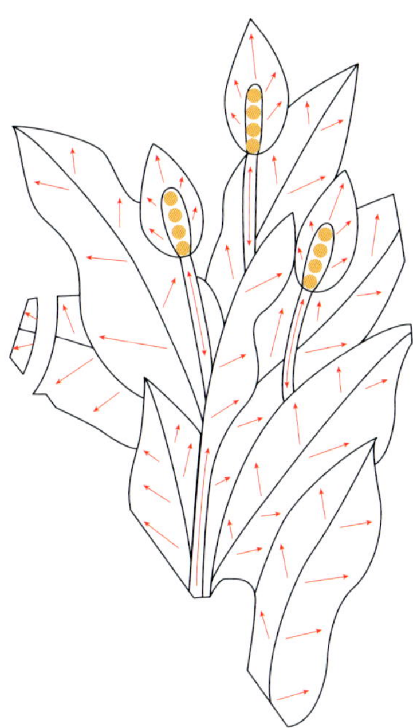

PLANTS

1. Satin stitch the peace lily leaves in 469, stitching from the center of the leaf diagonally up. Satin stitch the flowers in BLANC. Stitch 3–4 small French knots for the stamens in 782. **A B**

A

B

BACKGROUND

1. Split backstitch horizontal rows for the floor in 3721. Split backstitch vertical rows for the wall in 819. Stitch a little bit over the frame lines. **C D**

TIP • It's useful to actually draw stitch direction guidelines onto the fabric with the pen and ruler before you start stitching so you can keep the stitching straight.

C

D

Frames

1. Split backstitch the inner frame borders in BLANC following the direction of the rectangles. **A B**

2. Use padded satin stitch to stitch the frames. Use 6 strands of thread and 3–4 long stitches to pad each side of the frame, then cover the stitches in perpendicular satin stitches with 3 strands of thread. Stitch one frame in 938, another in 782, and a third in 991. **C D**

TIP • The frames are stitched with leftover thread from the table details, which both uses up the thread you have and adds cohesion to the piece. If you prefer, stitch the frames using the brown shades from the chairs.

3. Add fun extra details to the frames using spare thread:

- Stitch simple straight stitches of 745 on the inside of the brown frame. **E**
- Stitch zigzags in 3832 over the yellow frame. **F**
- Stitch French knots in 372 on the turquoise frame. **G**

5. Add the miniature frames. Glue them with textile glue, or attach them with a couple of couching stitches at each corner in a matching thread shade. H

6. Finish the hoop using your preferred finishing method (see Display and Finishing, page 36).

Make It Your Own!

The very nature of this gallery wall project makes it very easy to personalize and adapt. Using different miniature frames and stitching different tiny art will make the design your own.

WALLPAPER FABRIC

Instead of stitching the background, why not use a patterned base fabric that will act like a wallpaper! Just keep in mind this kind of fabric will be more difficult to paint onto, so maybe switch to adding miniature prints of famous art!

MAKE ART!

Mix up your gallery wall with different pieces of art and technique! How about beading, satin stitch, or even adding finished pieces of art of any medium!

Finished size: 8″ hoop

Cozy Crewel Study

Imagine curling up by the fire in an armchair with a sleepy dog at your feet, and a blazing fire in the hearth. Perfection! Using crewel thread to fill this design makes it feel so cozy! Embroidering with wool is a very different experience, and is sometimes called crewel wool embroidery.

TOOLS & MATERIALS

11½″ × 11½″ (29cm × 29cm) lightweight cotton linen fabric in a light neutral color

8″ (20cm) wooden embroidery hoop

Embroidery needle (size 3, 4, or 5)

Cozy Crewel Study Template (page 40)

THREAD

1 ball DMC pearl cotton, 310 (size 12)

DMC Eco Vita wool

- 001 (white)—1 skein
- 02 (pale pink)—1 skein
- 04 (grey)—1 skein
- 103 (dark brown)—1 skein
- 105 (mid brown)—1 skein
- 201 (pale yellow)—1 skein
- 203 (mustard yellow)—1 skein
- 205 (orange-brown)—1 skein
- 302 (peach-orange)—1 skein
- 408 (dark red)—1 skein
- 501 (red)—1 skein
- 604 (blue)—1 skein
- 704 (green)—1 skein
- 707 (pale green)—1 skein
- 708 (dark green)—1 skein

CREWEL WOOL

In this project, we use DMC Eco-Vita range, which is 100% natural dyed organic wool. All the colors are available in the DMC 30 skein collectors edition box if you prefer to purchase a set. Eco Vita Wool is made of two strands, but **do not separate** the strands. The wool is similar in thickness to 3 strands of 6-strand thread, so you shouldn't need a bigger needle. But, you might find size 3 or 4 more comfortable.

STITCHES USED

Split Backstitch (page 23)

Satin Stitch (page 23)

Outline

1. Load the fabric onto the hoop, and tighten the screw so the fabric tension is like the surface of a drum (see Prepare the Hoop, page 16).

2. Transfer the design onto the fabric (see Transfer Methods, page 18). I use the wash-away transfer paper method. **A**

3. Stitch all the outlines in split backstitch with 1 strand of 310 pearl thread. **B**

4. If you're using dissolvable transfer paper, remove the fabric from the hoop, and wash away the paper. Wait for the fabric to fully dry, iron it flat, then load the fabric back into the hoop. As you tighten, make sure that the straight lines of stitching are still straight.

5. Optional: If you plan to finish the project using the seal-in-the-hoop method (page 36), trim the outer skirt of fabric to 1″ (2.5cm). Then, using 1 strand of the 310 pearl thread, stitch around the outline circle with split backstitch, stitching through the fabric skirt. **C**

A

B

C

Color guide

205
203
002
105
103
105
704
205
604
302
103
707
201
302
201
105
004
004
203
205
707
302
203
704
103
103
002
408
201
203
604 & 302
604
501 & 408
708
501
707 & 302
203
408
105
203

Detail color guide

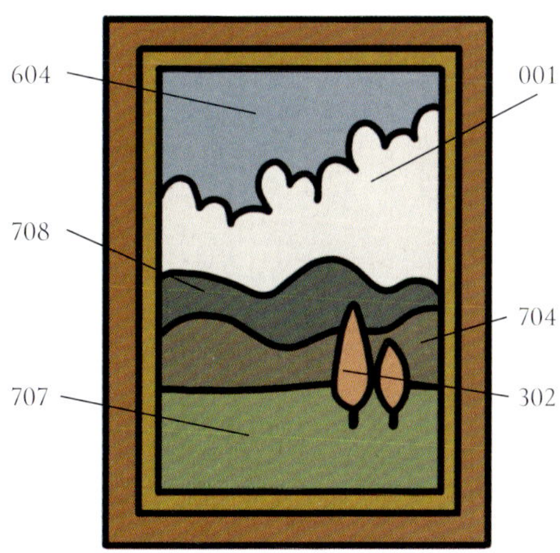

Fill Color

Don't split the strands of thread. Stay inside the stitched outlines. Refer to the color guides (page 103) and stitch direction guides in each section as needed. Unless otherwise stated, use split backstitch.

ARMCHAIRS

1. Stitch the wooden frames of both armchairs in 103. Stitch the green chair in 704, following the stitch direction guide. Repeat with the yellow chair in 203. **A** **B**

2. Stitch the cushions in 302 and 707. **C** **D**

TIP • Don't cut the lengths of crewel thread too long or pull the thread too tight while stitching to prevent the thread from fraying or breaking.

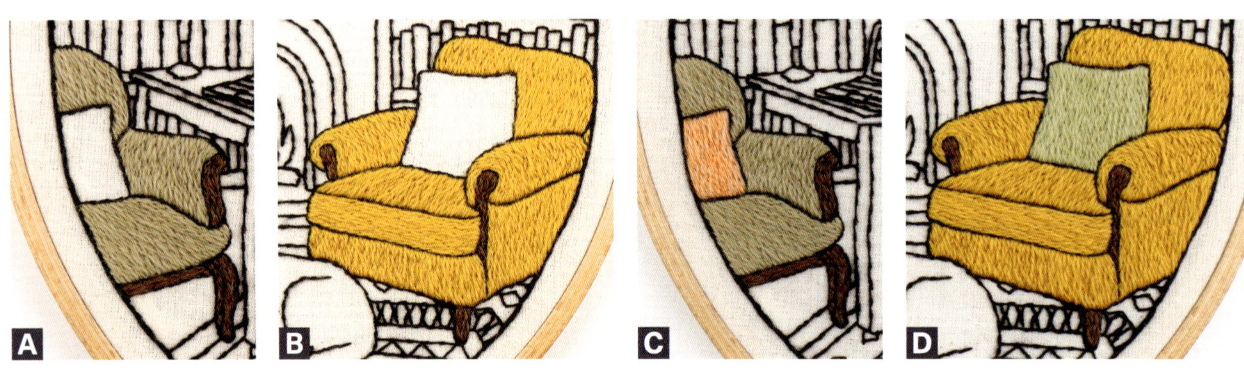
A B C D

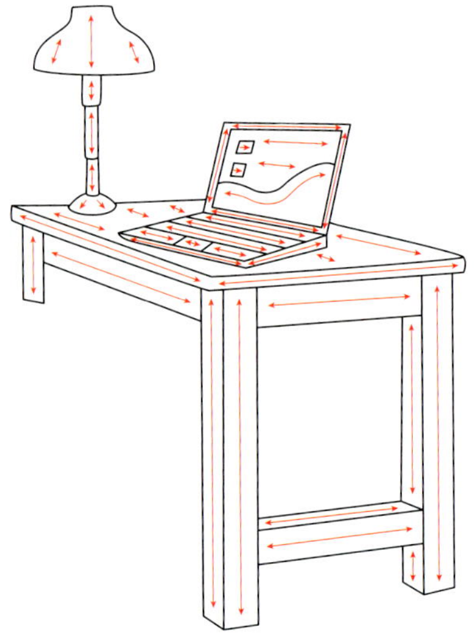

DESK

1. Stitch the table in 205. **E**

2. Stitch the lamp base in 203 and the shade in 201. Stitch the laptop in 004, then the desktop image in 707, 604, and 004. **F**

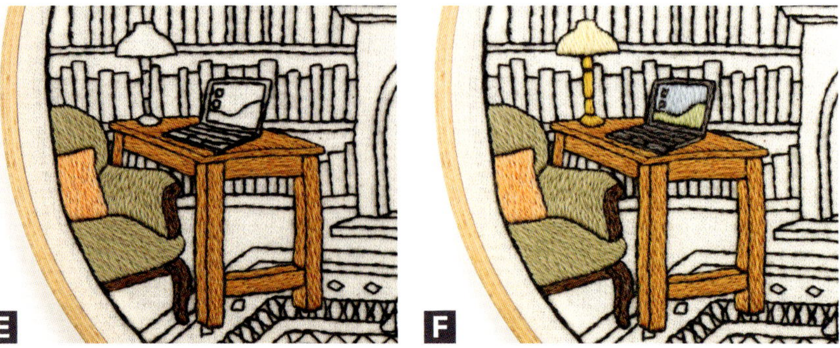
E F

FIREPLACE & PAINTING

1. Stitch the fire in 201 and 302. Stitch the logs in 105. Stitch the background in 103. **A**

2. Stitch the base in 004. Stitch the arch in 205 and 302. Stitch the rest of the fireplace in 704. Stitch the mantle in 105. **B**

3. Stitch the wall in 002. Stitch the frame in 205 and 203. **C**

4. Stitch the art following the color and stitch direction guides. **D**

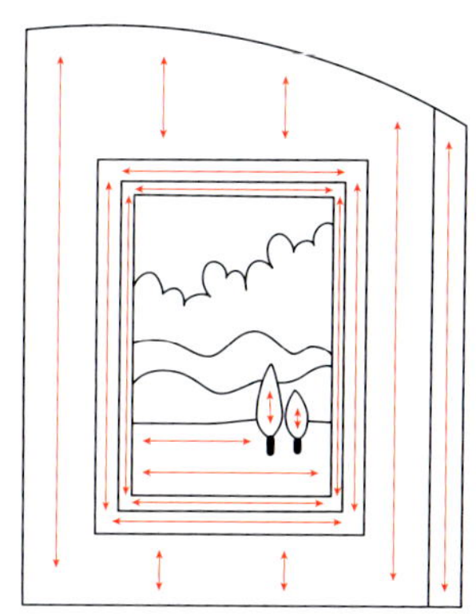

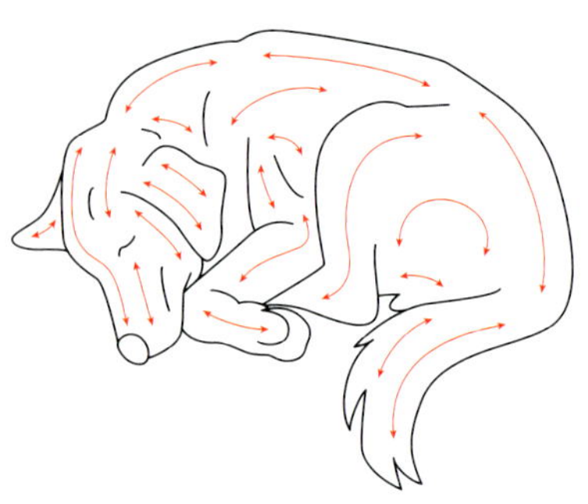

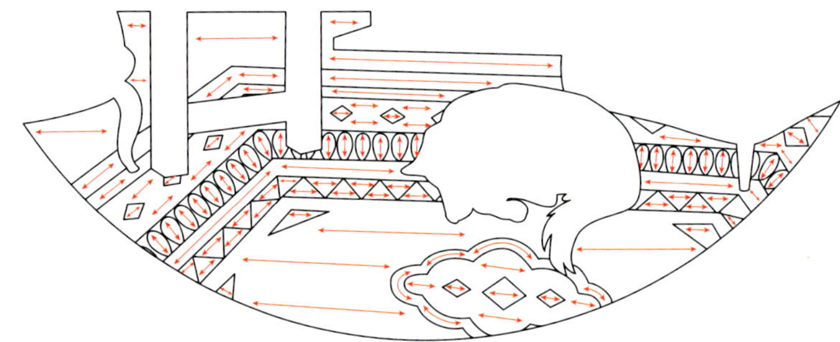

FLOOR

1. Stitch the dog in 201 with a 105 nose, following the fur direction. A

2. Stitch the rug in the following color order: B - H

3. Stitch the floor in 002. I

A

B 408

C 604

D 203

E 708

F 501

G 302

H 707

I 002

BOOKSHELVES

1. Stitch the shelves horizontally in 105. **A**

2. Satin stitch the back of the shelves vertically in 103. **B**

3. Satin stitch the books one color at a time. Follow the color guide or stitch at random, adding one or two books of each color onto each shelf.

4. Finish the hoop using your preferred finishing method (see Display and Finishing, page 36).

A

B

Make It Your Own!

TAPESTRY THREAD

Using chunky tapestry thread will make the piece even cosier! Enlarge the pattern and focus on a specific area.

ADD A READER

Draw a person reading on one of the chairs (see Customize the People, page 77). Change the rug to a checkerboard pattern, or make the picture above the fireplace more detailed.

Finished size: 7″ hoop

Miniature Music Room

Music is a wonderful part of life! Not many of us have the luxury of a dedicated music room, but in the world of embroidery there are no limits! This project is all about using miniature items alongside embroidery. You can search for miniature and dollhouse items online or at dollhouse shops. Pay attention to the scale of items and the perspective of the piece. An appropriate scale for miniatures to include with this design is 1:12.

TOOLS & MATERIALS

10½″ × 10½″ (26.7cm × 26.7cm) lightweight cotton linen fabric in a light neutral color

7″ (17.8cm) wooden embroidery hoop

Embroidery needle (size 5)

White craft glue/PVA glue

Tweezers

Miniatures:

- Dollhouse rug
- Ceramic "vase" beads
- Miniature leaves and dried flowers
- Halved miniature plant pot
- Miniature guitar

Miniature Music Room Template (page 40), printed on wash-away transfer paper

Music Sheet (page 40)

THREAD

1 ball DMC pearl cotton, 310 (size 12)

DMC 6-strand embroidery floss

- 311 (dark blue)—3 skeins
- BLANC (white)—1 skein
- 975 (mid brown)—1 skein
- 3826 (mid-pale brown)—1 skein
- 437 (pale brown)—1 skein
- 898 (dark brown)—1 skein
- 517 (bright blue)—1 skein
- 3857 (dark red)—1 skein
- 783 (mustard yellow)—1 skein
- 904 (or other green thread to match miniature leaves)—1 skein

STITCHES USED

Split Backstitch (page 23)

Couching Stitch (page 28)

Backstitch (page 22)

Beading (page 33)

Outline

1. Lay the miniature rug on the fabric at the same angle as the bottom of the piano. Pin it down if needed. Load the fabric and rug onto the hoop, and tighten the screw so the fabric tension is like the surface of a drum (see Prepare the Hoop, page 16). **A**

2. Transfer the design onto the fabric (see Transfer Methods, page 18). I use the wash-away transfer paper method. I recommend that method for this project because you won't be able to trace through the rug. **B**

3. Stitch all the outlines in split backstitch with 1 strand of 310 pearl thread, stitching over the rug. **C**

4. If you're using dissolvable transfer paper, remove the fabric from the hoop, and wash away the paper. Wait for the fabric to fully dry, iron it flat, then load the fabric back into the hoop. As you tighten, make sure that the straight lines of stitching are still straight.

5. Optional: If you plan to finish the project using the seal-in-the-hoop method (page 36), trim the outer skirt of fabric (including the rug) to 1″ (2.5cm). Then, using 1 strand of the 310 pearl thread, stitch around the outline circle with split backstitch, stitching through the fabric skirt. **D**

A

B

C

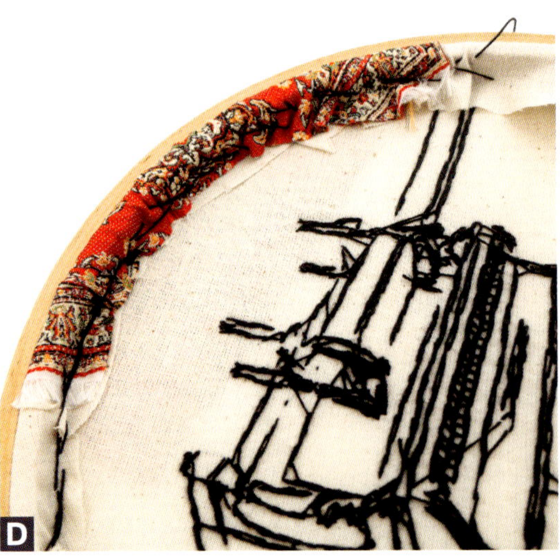
D

Color guide

TIP • Before using the pattern, gather your miniature items to see if they work with the scale of the pattern. If not, use a photocopier to scale the pattern up or down.

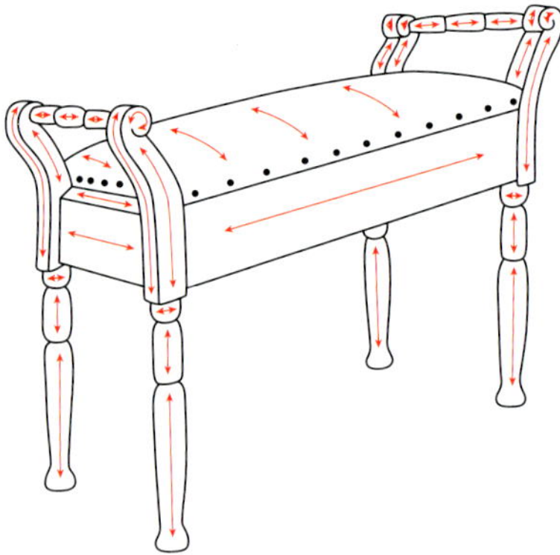

Fill Color

Unless otherwise stated, use 3 strands of embroidery floss to fill the color. Stay inside the stitched outlines. Refer to the color guide (page 113) and stitch direction guides in each section as needed.

PIANO

1. Split backstitch the light colored wood in 3826, referring to the stitch direction guide. **A**

2. Split backstitch the rest of the piano wood in 975. **B**

3. Straight stitch the keys in BLANC. Use tiny stitches, only one or two per piano key. Stitch the pedals in 783 and the feet in 898. **C**

5. Split backstitch the stool frame in 898. Split backstitch the stool cushion in 3857. **D**

BACKGROUND

1. Stitch horizontal rows of split backstitch for the floor in 437. Lift up the rug to stitch a little way under it. **A** **B**

2. Split backstitch the baseboards in 517. Stitch vertical rows of split backstitch for the wall in 311. **C**

A

B

C

TIP • Use the ruler and fineline pen to draw stitch guidelines before you begin stitching, referring to the stitch direction guide.

MINIATURE ELEMENTS

There are many ways to attach the miniature objects: glue, couching stitch, or even totally stitching over an object.

1. Arrange the miniatures as desired. When trying different formations, take photos and compare which looks the best. **A**

2. Stitch on the bead "vases" above the piano. **B**

3. Couch the leaf stems using 904 or a matching shade of green. Trim the stems to length. **C**

4. Use craft glue to attach the half plant pot and guitar. **D** **E**

TIP • A half plant pot makes things much easier for attaching to a flat surface. If you can't find one, cut a miniature basket in half. Or, draw in a plant pot and make it another stitched element!

5. Glue the ends of the dried flowers and arrange them into the bead vases. Use tweezers. **F**

6. Print the music sheet onto white paper, and cut it out. Attach the paper music onto the piano with a tiny line of backstitches through the centre. Use 1 strand of the 310 pearl thread or a matching shade of stranded thread. **G**

A

B

C

D

E

F

G

7. Finish the hoop using your preferred finishing method (see Display and Finishing, page 36).

Make It Your Own!

MINIATURE MANIA

The sky's the limit with this design! Use any cute miniatures you want! Enlarge the pattern to focus on a specific area. Change the rug and add a miniature vase to the right of the piano. It's really cool when the dried flowers emerge from the hoop!

FRAME IT!

The simplicity of this pattern makes it easy to change into a square design, perfect for framing in a shadow box frame. How about gluing on a shelf to the right of the piano, and filling the shadow box frame with interesting miniatures?!

Finished: 8″ hoop

Botanical Conservatory

Flowers are one of the most popular subjects of embroidery, and for good reason. There are so many varieties of shape, color, and texture, and likewise, there are plenty of interesting stitches and ways to create flowers in thread form! This fabulous conservatory pattern will show you a range of ways to stitch flowers, set against a gorgeous fabric backdrop for outside the windows.

TOOLS & MATERIALS

11½″ × 11½″ (29cm × 29cm) lightweight cotton or linen fabric for the background

8″ (20.3cm) unvarnished wooden embroidery hoop

Embroidery needle (size 5)

Lilac acrylic paint

Flat paintbrush

Sewing pin

Botanical Conservatory Template (page 40), printed on wash-away transfer paper

FABRIC

I'm using the fabric *Painterly Trees* by Clair Bremner for Robert Kaufman. I highly recommend using the wash-away transfer paper method (see Transfer Methods, page 18) since tracing is much harder to do and see on patterned fabric.

THREAD

1 ball DMC pearl cotton, 310 (size 12)

DMC 6-strand embroidery floss

- 437 (pale brown)—1 skein
- 975 (red-brown)—1 skein
- ECRU (pale cream)—1 skein
- 783 (mustard yellow)—1 skein
- 301 (terracotta orange)—1 skein
- 3033 (pale pink)—1 skein
- 07 (pink-grey)—1 skein
- 3041 (dark purple)—1 skein
- 154 (grape purple)—1 skein
- 3042 (pale purple)—1 skein
- 758 (pink)—1 skein
- 950 (pale yellow)—1 skein
- 580 (bottle green)—1 skein
- 470 (mid green)—1 skein
- 676 (yellow)—1 skein
- 3345 (dark green)—1 skein
- 372 (pale green)—1 skein
- 938 (dark brown)—1 skein
- 335 (rose pink)—1 skein

STITCHES USED

Straight Stitch (page 22)

Split Backstitch (page 23)

Satin Stitch (page 23)

Padded Satin Stitch (page 24)

Woven Wheel (page 30)

Basic Weave Stitch (page 28)

French Knots (page 25)

Woven Trellis (page 31)

Double Detached Chain Stitch (page 25)

Long and Short Stitch (page 33)

Turkeywork (page 27)

Couching Stitch (page 28)

Looped Bullion (page 26)

Preparing and Outline

1. Paint the outer ring of the embroidery hoop with the acrylic paint. Hold the hoop steady in one hand and paint around the screw, then paint the rest of the hoop. Wait for the paint to dry, then change where the hoop is held and finish painting the remaining area. Paint 2 coats, and let dry completely. **A**

2. Load the fabric onto the hoop, and tighten the screw so the fabric tension is like the surface of a drum (see Prepare the Hoop, page 16).

3. Transfer the design onto the fabric with the wash-away transfer paper method. **B**

4. Stitch all the outlines in split backstitch with 1 strand of 310 pearl thread. **C**

5. If you're using dissolvable transfer paper, remove the fabric from the hoop, and wash away the paper. Wait for the fabric to fully dry, iron it flat, then load the fabric back into the hoop. As you tighten, make sure that the straight lines of stitching are still straight.

6. Optional: If you plan to finish the project using the seal-in-the-hoop method (page 36), trim the outer skirt of fabric to 1˝ (2.5cm). Then, using 1 strand of the 310 pearl thread, stitch around the outline circle with split backstitch, stitching through the fabric skirt. **D**

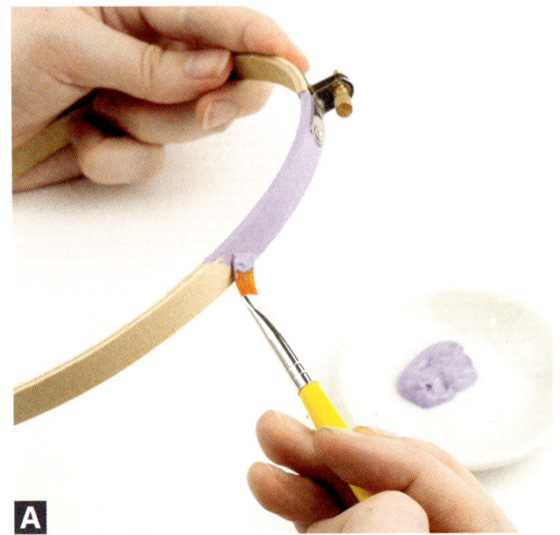
A

B

C

D

Color guide

ECRU
437
301
ECRU
07
3033
3041
758
3042
3042
950
758
975
ECRU
783
975
783
975
07
975

Fill Color

Unless otherwise stated, use 3 strands of embroidery floss to fill the color. Stay inside the stitched outlines. Refer to the color guide (page 121) and stitch direction guides in each section as needed.

WINDOWS

1. Split backstitch the window frames in 437. Each section will only need one or two rows of split backstitch. Stitch in the direction of the frames, referring to the stitch direction guide. **A**

2. Stitch the walls with horizontal rows of split backstitch in ECRU. **B**

A

B

FURNITURE

1. Split backstitch the coffee table, chair frames, and sofa frames in 975. **C**

C

D

E

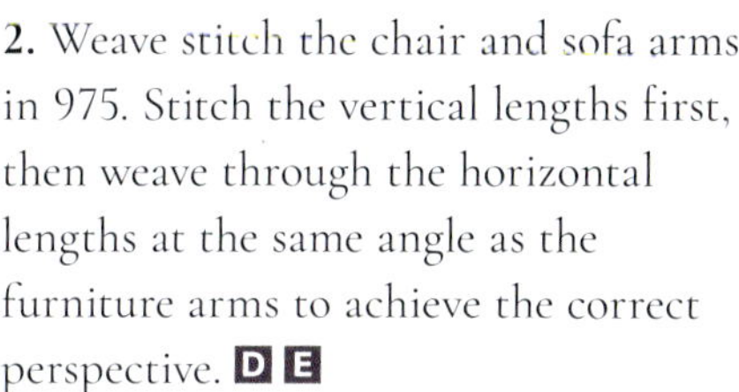

2. Weave stitch the chair and sofa arms in 975. Stitch the vertical lengths first, then weave through the horizontal lengths at the same angle as the furniture arms to achieve the correct perspective. D E

3. Split backstitch the yellow sofa cushions in 783. F

4. Fill the other cushions in 3042, 758, 3041, and 950 with padded satin stitch. For each cushion, stitch a few horizontal stitches in the center. Then, stitch vertical satin stitch on top. G H

F

G

H

A 301

PLANT POTS

1. Horizontally satin stitch all the pots and vases. Use one color at a time: **A** - **D**

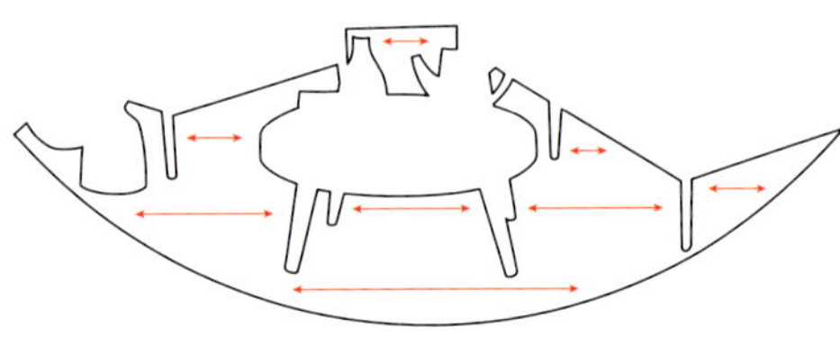

FLOOR

1. Stitch the floor with rows of horizontal split backstitch in 07. **E**

Flowers

Unlike the outlined windows and furniture, the flowers are freestyle, making them feel more organic and natural. However, if going freestyle makes you nervous, you can draw the shapes onto the fabric before stitching. Similarly, you might want to practice a new technique on a spare hoop before starting on the final piece. As the flowers build up, don't be afraid to stitch over the other flowers or previous stitching! Unless otherwise stated, use 3 strands of embroidery floss.

Flower placement diagram

Refer to the flower placement diagram for guidance on where to stitch each kind of flower.

WOVEN WHEEL ROSES: A

1. Straight stitch stems emerging from the top of the plant pot at different heights and angles in 580. At the top of one stem, stitch the woven wheel framework with five spokes in 758. **A**

2. Weave the rose, under one spoke then over the next, from the center to the outside. Use the needle to carefully arrange and fluff up the stitching. **B**

3. Repeat Step 2 for the other 2 stems. Repeat Steps 1–2 on the other A pot. **C**

A

B

C

FRENCH KNOT COW PARSLEY: B

1. Straight stitch branches emerging from the 2 B pots in 372. **A**
2. Stitch 4–5 smaller stems at the end of each branch using only two strands of thread. **B**
3. Add french knots in BLANC to the ends of all the stems, plus extra to fill out the branch. **C**

A

B

C

FRENCH KNOT LAVENDER: C

1. Straight stitch 5 stems emerging from the C pot in 3345. **D**
2. Stitch french knots around the stems in 3041. **E**

D

E

TURKEYWORK THISTLES: D

1. Stitch stems and some simple satin stitch leaves emerging from the D pots in 3345. A

2. Stitch three or four turkeywork loops at the top of each stem in 154. B

3. Couch stitch over the bottom half of the loops in 3345. C

4. Cut and fluff up the tassel flower. Repeat Steps 2–4 on the other pot. D

A

B

C

D

WOVEN TRELLIS LEAVES: E

TIP • Pin a scrap of paper behind the trellis framework to avoid catching the needle on other stitching.

1. Stitch the 3-stitch framework in 470 emerging from an E pot using the paper pin to hold it in place. E

2. Weave the leaves through the trellis lengths, starting at the top and working down. Remove the pin to complete the leaf. F

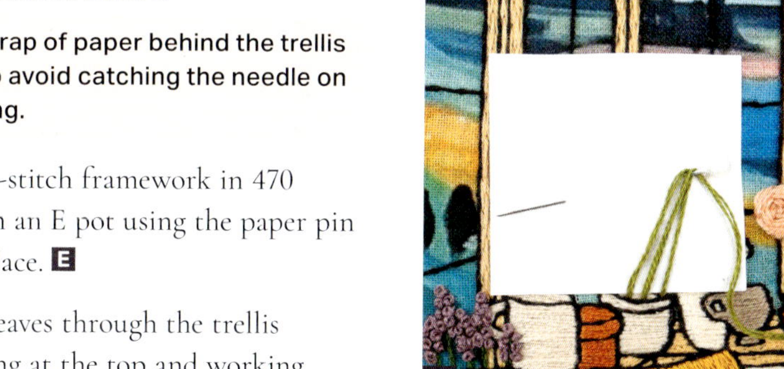
E

F

3. Fold down the leaf, and repeat Steps 1–2 to add 2 more leaves at different angles. Repeat Steps 1–2 on the other E pot, adding 2 leaves. G H

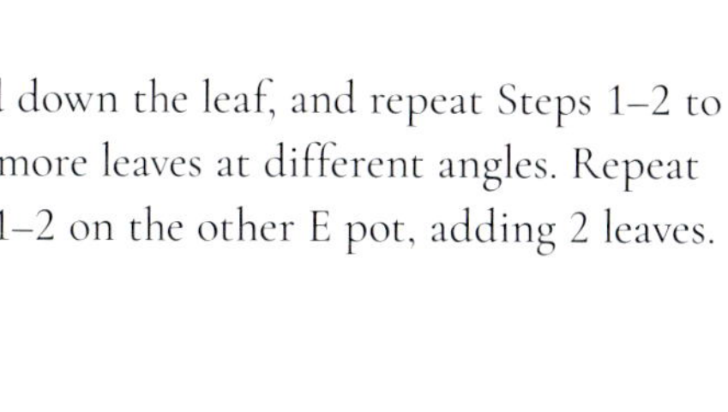

G

H

DOUBLE DETACHED CHAIN STITCH ASTERS: F

1. Split backstitch short stems in 470 in an F pot. **A**
2. Stitch the first layer of bigger detached chain stitch loops in 3042. Stitch 5 petals per flower. **B**
3. Stitch a smaller layer of detached chain stitch loops inside the first petals in 3042. **C**
4. Stitch a French knot in the middle of each petal in 783. Repeat Steps 1–4 in the other F pot. **E**

A

B

C

D

THREAD PAINTED PANSIES: G

It can be tricky to sketch or stitch over existing stitching. Stay patient and switch to fewer strands or a thinner needle if it is getting too hard to pull the needle through.

1. Sketch the flower shapes with a fineline or heat erasable pen in both G pots. **A**

2. Split backstitch the stems emerging from the pots in 372. **B**

3. Long and short stitch the outer layer of all petals in 3042. **C**

4. Long and short stitch the middle layer in BLANC. Layer a little over the stitches from Step 3, using alternating long and short stitches to blend. **D**

5. Long and short stitch the inner layer in 154. Again, overlap and blend with the Step 4 layer. **E** **F**

A

B

C

D

E

F

SUNFLOWERS: H

1. Split backstitch the stems emerging from the H pots at different angles and heights in 3345 (5 from the shelf pot, and 1 from the table pot). **A**

2. Stitch 1 French knot in 938 for the center of the flower. Then, stitch a ring of French knots around the first one. **B**

3. Straight stitch around the french knot center to form petals of slightly different lengths in 738. Stitch the petals close together. **C** **D**

A

B

C

D

LOOPED BULLION NERINE TULIPS: I

1. Straight stitch short stems emerging from the I pots in 470. **A**

2. Wrap 30–40 loops around the needle in 335 at the end of a stem. **B**

3. Pull the needle through the wrapped thread carefully. Keep gently pulling the thread as it bunches up, then bring the needle back through the fabric at the stem to form the loop. **C** **D**

4. Repeat 2–3 times to create the loopy nerine tulip shape over the stems. Repeat Steps 2–4 in the other I pot. **E**

A

B

C

D

E

TURKEYWORK GRASS: J

1. Stitch and anchor around 10 loops emerging from the J pots in 372. **A**
2. Trim and fluff the threads. **B**

STAR CROSS BLOSSOM: K

1. Split backstitch the stems emerging from a K pot in 938 as shown. **C**
2. Straight stitch small crosses all over the stems in 676. **D**
3. Stitch smaller crosses in 950 over the previous crosses and offset from them. **E**
4. Stitch little straight stitch leaves in the remaining spaces in 3345. Repeat Steps 1–4 in the second K pot. **F**

A

B

C

D

E

F

FISHBONE LEAF: L

1. Add a long straight stitch in 676, from the plant pot to where you want the top of the leaf to be. **A**

2. Alternating stitching from left to center and right to center, straight stitch a fishbone leaf pattern down to the bottom of the stem. Repeat to add other leaves. **B** **C**

3. Finish the hoop using your preferred finishing method (see Display and Finishing, page 36).

Make It Your Own!

UNIQUE FLOWERS

If you loved using different stitches to convey flowers, why not add your own ideas to the pots?

1. Source a photo of your chosen flower. Go through the Stitch Library (page 22), or research other embroidery stitches. Decide which stitches might convey the flower best. **A**

2. Practice working out your design in a spare hoop! **B**

3. Add the new flower design to your embroidery! Here, the pattern has been enlarged to focus on the left side of the conservatory. The plants are a mix of woven trellis leaves, turkey work grass, couched dried flowers, and the new daffodil design.

CHANGE SCENES

The fabric background is so important for this design! Change to a wintry or a forest scene for a completely different feel! Add miniature plants to the pots to create a very 3D piece. Add white french knots to the windows to look like snow!

Finished size: 7″ hoop

Colorful Kid's Bedroom

Children's bedrooms are surely the most fun rooms in the house! They are full of color and things to do. This project uses patterned fabric and added miniature elements to create a funky, rainbow bedroom. I highly recommend using the wash-away transfer paper method (see Transfer Methods, page 18) since tracing is much harder to do and see on patterned fabric. Striped fabric is a great option for the floor, as it can mimic the look of floorboards.

TOOLS & MATERIALS

10½″ × 10½″ (26.7cm × 26.7cm) lightweight yellow gingham fabric

10½″ × 6″ (26.7cm × 15.2cm) lightweight printed fabric (for the floor)

2″ × 2¾″ (5cm × 7cm) rectangle of faux fur

1–2 scraps of printed fabric

7″ (17.8cm) unvarnished wooden embroidery hoop

Embroidery needle (size 5)

Yellow acrylic paint

Flat paintbrush

1–2 miniature books

12 colored pom-poms (3/16″ or 5mm)

Craft glue

Colorful Kid's Bedroom Template (page 40), printed on wash-away transfer paper

THREAD

1 ball DMC pearl cotton, 310 (size 12)

DMC 6-strand embroidery floss

- 433 (dark brown)—1 skein
- 3828 (pale brown)—1 skein
- 739 (pale yellow)—1 skein
- 3859 (dusty pink)—1 skein
- 3052 (dusty green)—1 skein
- BLANC (white)—1 skein
- 746 (pale cream)—1 skein
- 948 (pale pink)—1 skein

STITCHES USED

Split Backstitch (page 23)

Satin Stitch (page 23)

French Knots (page 25)

Chain Stitch (page 24)

Couching Stitch (page 28)

Blanket Stitch (page 35)

ABC

Preparing and Outline

1. Paint the outer ring of the embroidery hoop with the acrylic paint. Hold the hoop steady in one hand and paint around the screw, then paint the rest of the hoop. Wait for the paint to dry, then change where the hoop is held and finish painting the remaining area. Paint 2 coats, and let dry completely. **A**

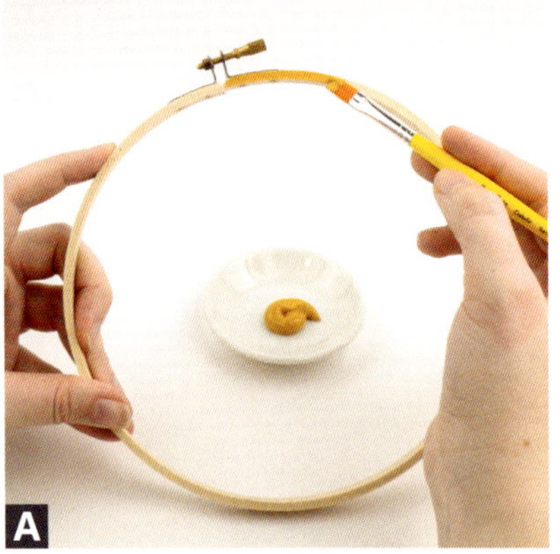

2. Lay the gingham fabric right side up. Lay the floor fabric on top (right side up), covering the bottom third of the gingham. Fold the top raw edge of the fabric under, and press with an iron or your finger. **B**

3. Load both fabrics onto the hoop, and tighten the screw so the fabric tension is like the surface of a drum (see Prepare the Hoop, page 16).

4. Transfer the design onto the fabric with the wash-away transfer paper method. Carefully place the pattern so that the join between fabrics will be covered by the furniture stitching. **C**

5. Stitch all the outlines in split backstitch with 1 strand of 310 pearl thread. **D**

6. Remove the fabric from the hoop, and wash away the transfer paper. Wait for the fabric to fully dry, iron it flat, then load the fabric back into the hoop. As you tighten, make sure that the straight lines of stitching are still straight.

7. Optional: If you plan to finish the project using the seal-in-the-hoop method (page 36), trim the outer skirt of fabric to 1˝ (2.5cm). Then, using 1 strand of the 310 pearl thread, stitch around the outline circle with split backstitch, stitching through the fabric skirt. **E**

Color guide

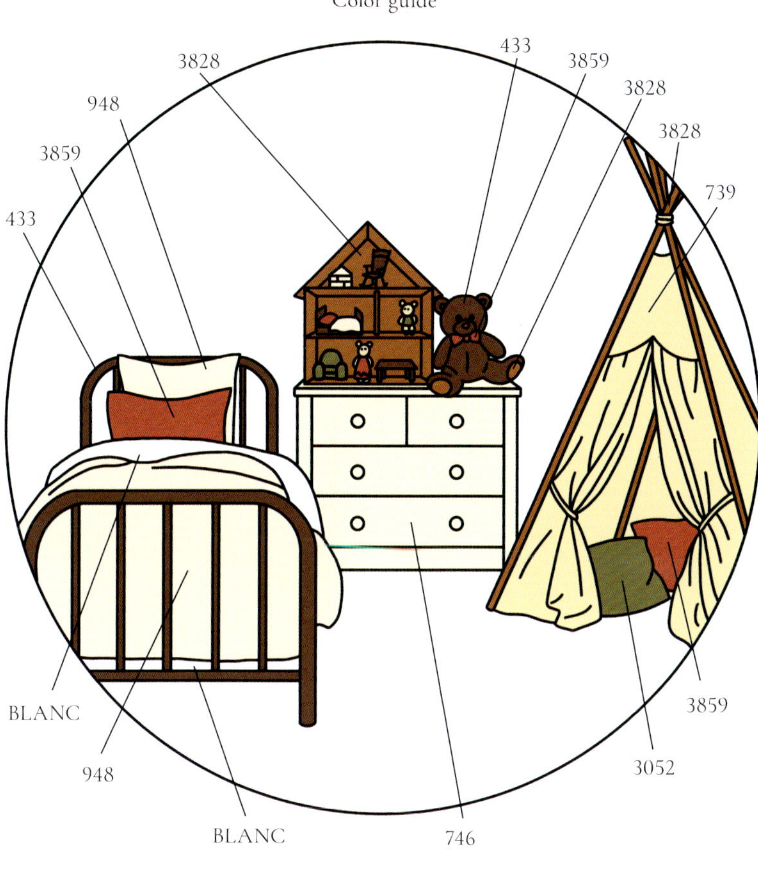

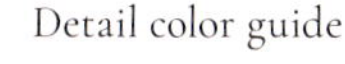

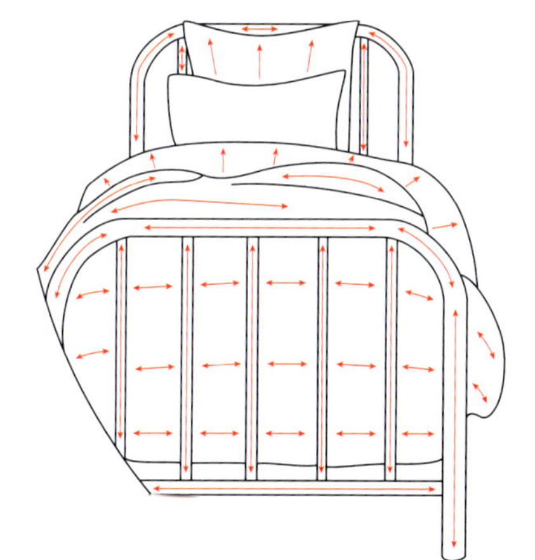

Fill Color

Unless otherwise stated, use 3 strands of embroidery floss to fill the color. Stay inside the stitched outlines. Refer to the color guides (above) and stitch direction guides in each section as needed.

BED

1. Split backsitch the bed frame in 433. Fill the front pillow with French knots in 3859. Satin stitch the back pillow in 948. **A**

A

2. Stitch the folded top of the duvet and the sheet at the bottom of the bed in BLANC. Use vertical satin stitch for the duvet top and horizontal satin stitch for the sheet between the bed frame bars. Split backstitch the duvet in 948. **B**

TIP • The small horizontal stitches for the sheet and duvet between the bars of the bed take a long time to stitch. If you stitch them with vertical split backstitches to save time, it won't be too noticeable!

B

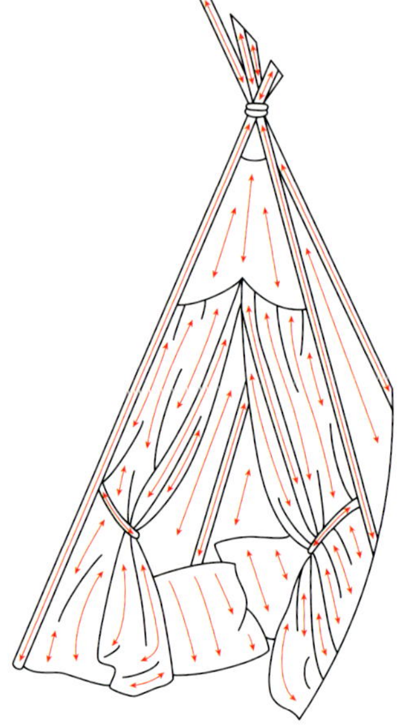

READING TENT

1. Split backstitch the tent frame in 3828. **A**
2. Split backstitch the tent canvas and frame tie in 739, following the stitch direction guide. **B**
3. Split backstitch the right-side cushion in 3859. **C**
4. Chain stitch the left-side cushion in 3052. **D**

A

B

C

D

DRAWERS & DOLLHOUSE

1. Stitch the chest of drawers in 746, using both vertical and horizontal split backstitch according to the stitch direction guide. **A**

2. Split backstitch the teddy bear fur in 433. Satin stitch the soles of its feet in 3828. Satin stitch the bow tie and nose in 3859. **B**

3. Satin stitch the dollhouse in 3828, carefully stitching around the accessories. **C**

4. Satin stitch the dollhouse accessories in various colors from other parts of the bedroom, referring to the color guide as desired. The parts are so tiny they will only need one or two stitches to fill. **D**

Extra Elements

1. Cut out 1 rectangle ¾″ × 1″ (1.9cm × 2.5cm), and 1 square 1″ × 1″ (2.5cm × 2.5cm) square from the scrap fabric and arrange them on the wall. Secure them down with a straight stitch in each corner using the pearl outline thread. **A**

2. Couch stitch the edges of the fabric to create the frames around the rectangles. Use 3052 and 3859, or choose colors as desired. 433 or other brown shades are a great option to create wooden-effect frames. **B C**

3. Optional: If you're using a solid color fabric, embroider *ABC* (or desired phrase). I'm using 3 strands of 948 and couching stitch. **D**

4. Cut the fur fabric into a small oval, 1⅜" x 2⅛″ (3.5 × 5.4cm). Blanket stitch the fabric to the floor with 746 or a matching color. **E**

5. Glue miniature books onto the rug and floor by the reading tent. **F**

6. Make a string of colored pom-poms. Thread the needle with black pearl thread, then pierce the center of all 12 pom-poms, stringing them together. Leave about 5mm between each pom pom. Leave 6″ (15.2cm) of thread on each end. **G**

A

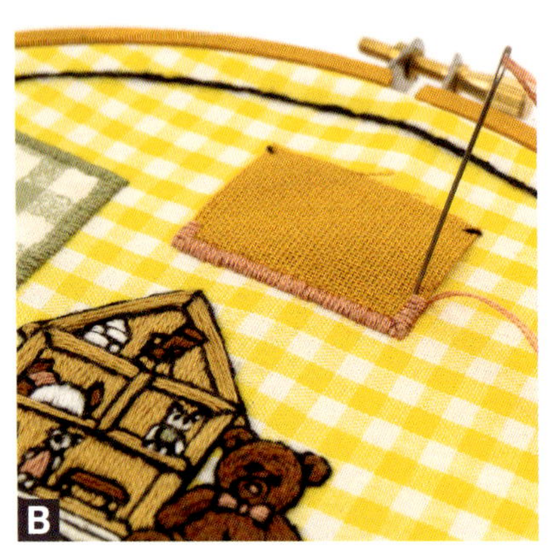
B

C

D

E

F

G

7. Attach the pom-pom garland. Stitch one end of the garland to the back side of the hoop through the outline of the piece on one side. Stitch four small straight stitches on top of the circular outline to anchor the garland. Loosely drape the garland to the other side of the circle, and repeat. Lift the center of the garland to the top of the circle, then stitch it in place with one small straight stitch. Adjust the pom-poms so they are evenly spread. **H**

8. Finish the hoop using your preferred finishing method (see Display and Finishing, page 36).

Make It Your Own!

DESIGN CHOICES

The colors for this room are fairly neutral, but using different color gingham, specific books, as well as different thread choices, you can change the bedroom into a specific kid's paradise! Also, consider changing the pom pom garland for a string of cute felt flags!

WHO LIVES HERE?

Instead of adding the fabric frames above the bed, embroider a name and turn the embroidery into an adorable bedroom sign!

Finished size: 7˝ hoop

Stained Glass Entryway

The final project in this book is actually the first thing people see in any house! This front hallway is full of color and life, and importantly, full of light. Cutting into embroidery can seem daunting, but by following this project and adding wire to the reverse side, you can create a stunning, stained glass entryway scene.

TOOLS & MATERIALS

10½˝ × 10½˝ (26.7cm × 26.7cm) lightweight cotton linen fabric in a neutral color

7˝ (17.8cm) unvarnished wooden embroidery hoop

Embroidery needle (size 5)

Red acrylic paint

Flat paintbrush

Aluminium jewelry/craft wire (0.8mm), approx 30" (76.2cm)

Wire snips

White craft glue/PVA glue

6˝ × 8˝ (15.2cm × 20.3cm) rectangle of thick clear 240 micron PVC acetate

Permanent markers in a variety of colors

Tape

Stained Glass Entryway Template and Stained Glass Template (page 40)

THREAD

1 ball DMC pearl cotton, 310, size 12

DMC 6-strand embroidery floss

- BLANC (white)—1 skein
- 666 (red)—1 skein
- 945 (pale peach)—1 skein
- 729 (orange-brown)—1 skein
- 3826 (brown)—1 skein
- 334 (blue)—1 skein
- 645 (dark grey)—1 skein
- 356 (dusty pink)—1 skein
- 898 (dark brown)—1 skein
- 732 (pale bottle green)—1 skein
- 733 (bottle green)—1 skein
- 3771 (peach)—2 skeins

STITCHES USED

Split Backstitch (page 23)

Satin Stitch (page 23)

Couching Stitch (page 28)

Detached Chain Stitch (page 25)

Woven Wheel (page 30)

French Knots (page 25)

Preparing and Outline

1. Paint the outer ring of the embroidery hoop with the acrylic paint. Hold the hoop steady in one hand and paint around the screw, then paint the rest of the hoop. Wait for the paint to dry, then change where the hoop is held and finish painting the remaining area. Paint 2 coats, and let dry completely. **A**

2. Load the fabric onto the hoop, and tighten the screw so the fabric tension is like the surface of a drum (see Prepare the Hoop, page 16).

3. Transfer the design onto the fabric (see Transfer Methods, page 18). I use the wash-away transfer paper method. **B**

4. Stitch all the outlines in split backstitch with 1 strand of 310 pearl thread. **C**

TIP • Be careful not to stitch any thread at the back across the window spaces which will get cut out!

5. If you're using dissolvable transfer paper, remove the fabric from the hoop, and wash away the paper. Wait for the fabric to fully dry, iron it flat, then load the fabric back into the hoop. As you tighten, make sure that the straight lines of stitching are still straight.

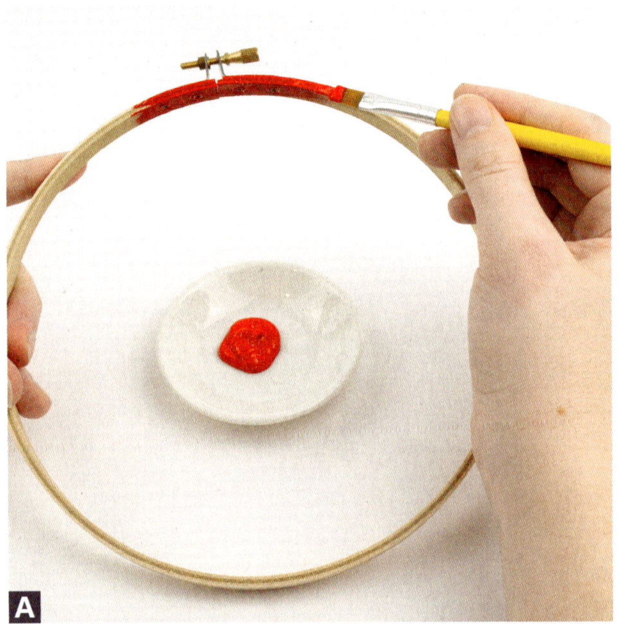

A

B

C

6. Optional: If you plan to finish the project using the seal-in-the-hoop method (page 36), trim the outer skirt of fabric to 1″ (2.5cm). Then, using 1 strand of the 310 pearl thread, stitch around the outline circle with split backstitch, stitching through the fabric skirt. **D**

Color guide

666
3826
729
945
3771
666
945
356
356
666
898
733
732
645
729
BLANC
898
898
BLANC
BLANC & 666
334
645
BLANC

Add the Wire

1. Bend the thin wire into rectangles that match the shape of the door frame, window panels, and door windows (which will all be cut out). Make 3 separate pieces: 2 small rectangles for the door windows, and 1 large piece for the frame windows.

Using the outline or the pattern as a template, bend the wire with the wire snips to create corners. When the shape is complete, cut the wire with the snips. For the large wire piece, it doesn't matter exactly which way you bend the wire, but there should be at least one piece of wire on all sides of the windows. There can be overlapping wires if you need. **A** **B**

2. Attach the door panel wires to the back of the hoop using couching stitches in 666 (the same color as the door). Attach the window panel wires with 3862. **C**

TIP • Don't worry too much about how the couching stitches look on the right side; they will be covered up. Just stay inside the outlines on the front.

A

B

C

Fill Color

Unless otherwise stated, use 3 strands of embroidery floss to fill the color. Stay inside the stitched outlines. Refer to the color guide (page 147) and stitch direction guides in each section as needed.

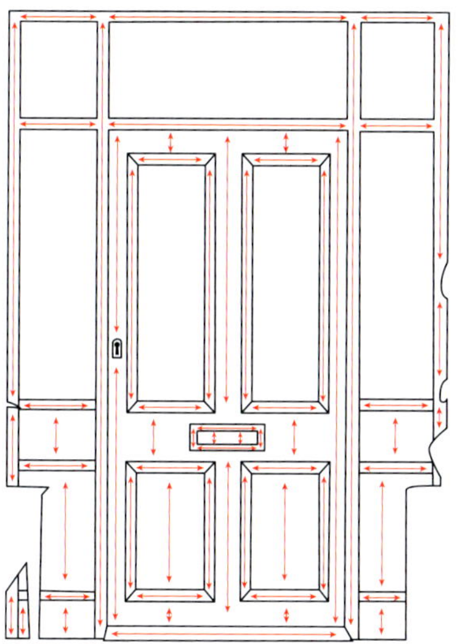

DOOR

1. Split backstitch the door in 666. It can be tricky to stitch around the wire. Angle the needle in different ways to avoid it. **A**

2. Split backstitch the door frame in 3826 to stitch the door frame. As with the outlines, take care not to let threads cross the windows across the back of the hoop. **B**

3. Satin stitch the letterbox and lock details in 729. **C**

A

B

C

UMBRELLA STAND

1. Split backstitch the umbrella stand in BLANC. A

2. Add freehand detached chain stitch flower petals and french knots in 334. Split backstitch the top and bottom stripes. B

3. Satin stitch the umbrellas in 645 and the handles in 898. C

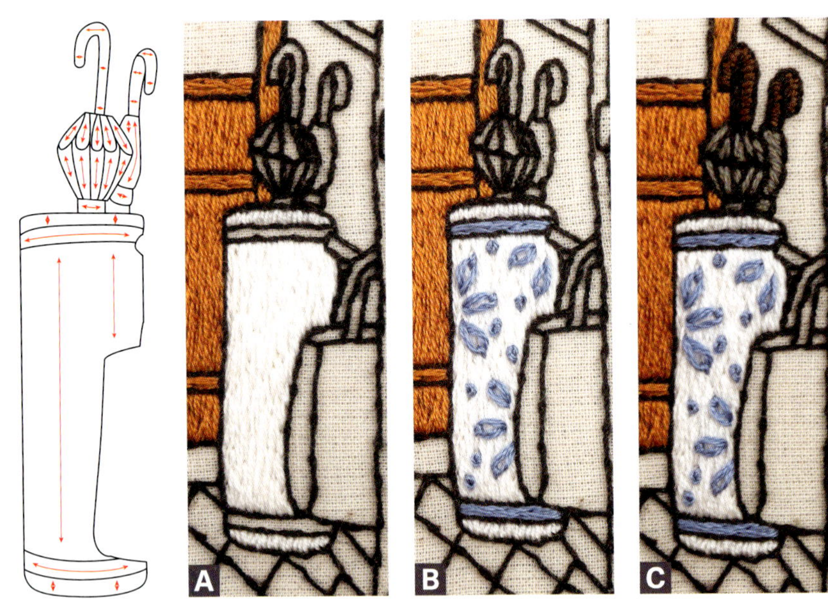

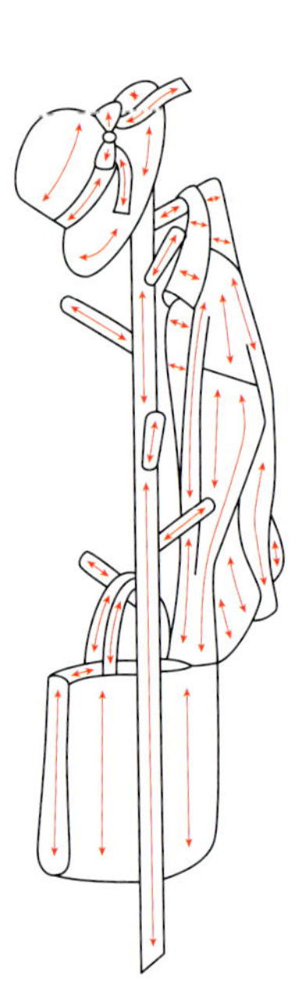

COAT STAND

1. Split backstitch the wooden coat stand in 729. D

2. Split backstitch the coat in 356. Refer to the stitch direction guide to create the drape of the coat. E

3. Split backstitch the hat in 945, with 666 for the ribbon. Split backstitch the bag with 898. F

TABLE

1. Split backstitch the table in 898. A

2. Split backstitch the vase in BLANC. Add detached chain stitch petals and french knots in 334 to match the umbrella stand. B

3. Split backstitch the stems and leaves in 732 and 733. C

4. Stitch french knot flowers in 945 on the top three open areas. D

5. Stitch mini woven wheel roses in the circles in 356. E

6. Satin stitch the lilies in 666. Stitch satin stitch envelopes in BLANC, plus a couple of stitches in 666 for the stamp. F

A

B

C

D

E

F

A

BACKGROUND & FLOOR

1. Satin stitch the tiles in BLANC and 645. A

2. Split backstitch the edges of the tile floor in BLANC. Split backstitch the baseboards in 3826. B

3. Fill the background walls with vertical rows of split backstitch in 3771. Draw guidelines with a ruler and pen before stitching to help keep the rows straight. C

B

C

Windows

CUT FABRIC

1. Using sharp snips, cut a straight line into the center of each window. Then, cut from the line to each corner, right up to the stitching. **A**

2. Carefully cut the fabric out, cutting right along the edges of each window, but not cutting through any stitching. **B**

3. Paint craft glue onto the edges of the fabric to prevent fraying. Wait for the glue to dry, then draw on the edges with a black permanent marker. **C** **D**

A

B

C

D

STAINED GLASS

1. Tape a piece of the transparent plexiglass/plastic on top of the printed Stained Glass template. A

2. Use a black permanent marker to trace the stained glass outline. Wait for the black to dry, then fill the design using colored permanent markers. B C

TIP • The colors might look very bright against a white background, but once you hold the plastic up to the light, the colors will look more subtle and natural!

3. Cut the sheet to fit inside the back of the hoop. Align with the window spaces, then add craft glue around the edges. Glue in place. D

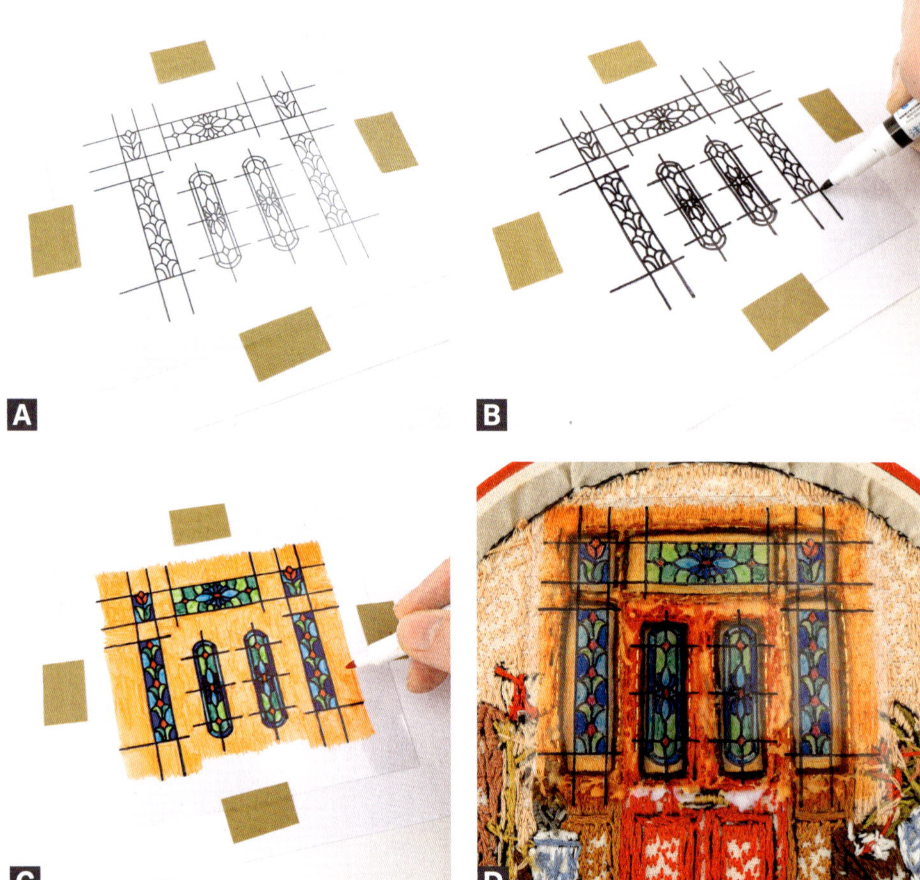

Make It Your Own!

WHAT'S OUTSIDE?

You don't have to use stained glass! How about adding a photo behind the hoop? Stitch just the doorway into an oval hoop.

OPEN THE DOOR!

If you're feeling really brave, stitch a separate door with wire around the edges, cut it out, then stitch it to the side of the doorframe so that the door can actually open and close!

Mix-And-Match Interiors

Introduction to Making Embroidery Patterns

If you've enjoyed using the patterns in this book, why not take the next step and design your own unique embroidery pattern? The rooms I design are made of three elements: the fixed wall, floor, and ceiling, the large furniture items, and then all the little details which fill the space and make it into a cozy home.

To start you on this journey, you'll find over 25 templates for living room elements, from big furniture, to accessories like books, plants, and pets. Use these to mix-and-match and create your own pattern!

MATERIALS

Wash-Away transfer paper

Scissors

Sheet of paper

Pencil and ruler

Embroidery hoop of choice

DMC 310 pearl thread

DMC 6-stranded embroidery thread in colors of choice

Fabric of choice

Pen (optional)

Mix-and-Match Templates (page 40)

Using the Mix-and-Match Templates

1. Transfer the pattern elements onto wash-away transfer paper (see Transfer Methods, page 18).

TIP • Use a photocopier to your advantage! Copy in reverse to flip the direction of the pieces. Scale the copy to make the pieces bigger or smaller.

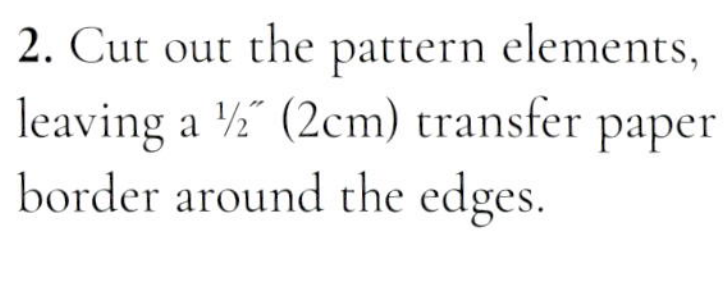

2. Cut out the pattern elements, leaving a ½˝ (2cm) transfer paper border around the edges.

3. Trace the size of the hoop onto paper. Draw 3 lines with a pencil to create the walls and floor to help create the room's perspective. Look at photos of rooms or your own home for inspiration. You don't need to actually stitch these lines in the final piece if you don't want them. Use a pencil so you can change if needed. Add baseboards if you want them.

4. Have fun arranging the cut-out elements into cute scenes! You don't need to use all the elements in one pattern. Start with the bigger pieces, then add the smaller elements on top. Don't be afraid to layer the pieces. **A**

A

TIP • **Keep all the cut out elements that you haven't used yet in a sealed bag in a dry place, so you can use them for other embroideries later!**

5. Once you are happy with the arrangement, trace the wall and floor lines onto the fabric (as desired), and stick the elements on. You can also draw in your own elements such as extra ornaments, people, or scenery. You could even add seasonal designs such as a Christmas tree or flag bunting to create a themed scene! **B** **C** **D**

B

C

D

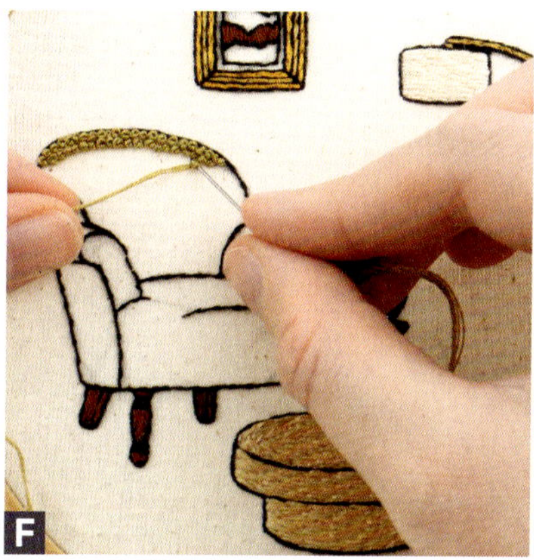

6. Stitch the outlines. Keep in mind which elements are in front of others. E

7. Dissolve the transfer paper, and stitch the color. Think about the stitched elements and which stitches would make interesting textures (refer to the Stitch Library, page 22). Make sure to pay attention to stitch direction, using the stitch direction guides in each project as reference. F

8. Add extra miniature elements as desired or use one of the special techniques in this book to make the embroidery piece even more unique and interesting! G

About the Author

Originally from Southampton, England, Penny holds a degree in fashion from Bournemouth Arts College. She now calls Taipei, Taiwan home, where she balances life as a teacher by day with her passionate pursuit of embroidery whenever time allows.

Penny discovered embroidery over a decade ago after completing her formal education, developing a distinctive illustrative style characterized by bold outlines and vibrant color blocking. Her work stands out through its bright palette, inviting designs, and rich textures created through varied stitching techniques and miniature elements.

Her art celebrates the beauty found in everyday domestic scenes and cozy interiors, while drawing inspiration from her global travels and the diverse places she has called home. Penny has exhibited her work in both Bournemouth and Taipei, led embroidery workshops, and shares her craft internationally through her kits and patterns.

Visit Penny online and follow on social media!

Website: pennydowdell.com

Instagram: @pennydowdell

Pinterest: /pennydowdell

Facebook: /travelandembroidery